The

RULES

of the

GAME

Pierluigi

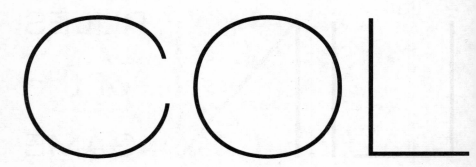

COL

Translated from the Italian by Iain Halliday

Steve

Happy Birthday

Maybe some of his tips on dealing
with difficult situations may be of
assistance in your role of mediator.

Best wishes
Andy & Carole

LINA

The RULES of the GAME

MACMILLAN

First published 2003 by Macmillan
an imprint of Pan Macmillan Ltd
Pan Macmillan, 20 New Wharf Road, London N1 9RR
Basingstoke and Oxford
Associated companies throughout the world
www.panmacmillan.com

ISBN 1 4050 3279 0

A CIP catalogue record for this book is available from
the British Library.

Printed and bound in Great Britain by
Mackays of Chatham plc, Chatham, Kent

For Francesca and Carolina

Contents

Illustrations

Manchester United–Real Madrid 2003 (© John Peters)
Warming up (© Glyn Kirk/ Action Plus)
Training with other referees in 1998 (© PA Photos/ EPA)
Offering my consolations to Stefan Effenberg (© Getty Images)
Testing Perugia's waterlogged pitch (© Getty Images)
With Gilles Veissiere before Euro 2000 (© PA Photos/ EPA)
Receiving my trophy as world's best referee, 2000 (© PA Photos/ EPA)
At the fitness test for the 2002 World Cup (© PA Photos/ EPA)
With David Beckham during Argentina–England (© PA Photos/ EPA)
My 'team' before the 2002 World Cup final (© Getty Images)
Refereeing the final, 2002 (© PA Photos/ EPA)
With Sepp Blatter at the end of the final (© PA Photos/ EPA)
Sportsmanship is important even at the highest level (© John Peters)
Controlling the situation, Champions' League, 2002 (© John Peters)
At the *Donna Sotto le Stelle* fashion show, July 2002 (© PA Photos/ EPA)

Introduction

'I can see you, my son, in front of the television engrossed in the cartoons (*Tweety-Pie and Sylvester, Captain Tsubasa, Tom and Jerry*) and in the football matches. We sit on the sofa together and you immediately ask me about the referee. Maybe it's because when he's dressed in yellow he grabs your attention, just like the characters from the cartoons. You're more interested in him than the players – Buffon the goalkeeper with his pink shirt, Ronaldo with his bald head, Adriano with his earring. You like watching the man who has to decide, instantly, on a penalty, an offside, a foul. And it's on him – the man who couldn't make it as a footballer – that the people on the terraces unload all the week's resentment, all their anger in defeat.

'In football there are many solitary roles that have found a place in literature: the right wing, which became the title of a work of poetry by Fernando Acitelli; the centre-forward's story, as told by Soriano; the goalkeeper's, recounted by Dino Zoff. But the man who's really alone is him, my son, the referee who brings a smile to your face when he puts on his yellow strip.

'I've known several referees over the course of my career, and I've found a sadness in all of them, a sadness that's never been revealed before: it comes from those difficult first years, for example, refereeing on pitches where there's no protection, no security, refereeing lads who don't yet shave and are bullied by furious fathers, obsessed managers and violent, disrespectful players. Many of these referees bear scars on their faces from punches, bottles and stones thrown. Absurd stories – being locked up for hours in the dressing room after matches, escaping in car boots just as spies do in the movies. It all makes you want to say enough is enough. Is it worth risking one's life for a derisory sum of money, for no fame and for an often misspelled mention in the results in the local papers? But no referee is born by pure chance, it's a conscious decision that involves passion and martyrdom and a belief in the rules. And that's the way these lonely men keep going, dreaming of reaching Serie A or of refereeing a World Cup final.

'I'll always feel for those youngsters – and they still exist today – who go off to referee in the trenches, their only protection their own courage. Youngsters who rather than go for a trip in a boat or for a night out at the cinema with friends, choose to dedicate them-selves to making sure that the secular rite we watch together from the sofa starts in perfect time. We're ready to celebrate when our team scores or to be sad about that goal, which, all things con-sidered, could have been avoided. Without the referee football wouldn't have any sense – you can play without a goalkeeper or a centre-forward, but not without the man who runs and runs and runs without ever touching the ball. He never scores. He never ever receives heartfelt applause. A long round of applause. An applause to bring you out in goose bumps.'

I took these lines from Darwin Pastorin's latest book, *Lettera a mio figlio sul calcio* (*A Letter to my Son About Football*), because it seemed to be the best way to start writing about my world – the world of the referee.

So who are they really, these people so varied in terms of age, of sex, of culture, of class, who share such a love for sport that they dedicate their time to the service of those who actually play it? And I'm not just talking about football referees, though they are obviously those I know best, this includes other sports as well – basketball, volleyball, rugby, track and field judges and timekeepers, tennis umpires and line judges and so the list goes on.

The eye of television, or rather television's many eyes, essentially means that there are no secrets during the ninety or so minutes of a football match. It misses nothing, everything is seen and judged. But this is not the same for us. It's a bit like talking about an iceberg. The mass of ice above the water is so big that it makes you think there's nothing beneath it. But it's really what you don't see, what is below the water, that's even bigger.

And that's the way it is for us. Everyone knows us because of what we do for ninety minutes, yet few, very few, know who we are, what we do, what we think about when we're off the pitch.

So it's worth trying to explain it, in the hope that this knowledge will help improve relationships and help us understand and appreciate the role of the referee more.

By doing this we could free ourselves, for example, of a series of clichéd prejudices– such as the widespread theory that the best referee is the one who gets himself noticed the least.

I've often wondered why that should be, without ever coming up with an explanation. After all, refereeing isn't about playing hide and seek . . .

Perhaps it would be closer to the truth to say that the best referee is the one who makes the least number of mistakes, but that's such a hackneyed concept that we take it for granted.

So let's speak about courage, about the courage to decide, to take difficult, important decisions, so important that they put the referee in a situation where he does get noticed, where he becomes *a* leading character, but not *the* leading character in a match.

The best referee is the referee who has this conviction, the one who makes the decisions even when it would be easier not to, putting the problem off until later, until the end of the match.

This is the most important quality a referee can have, and my advice to anyone just starting out is to learn from the very beginning to have that courage.

One

My World Cup

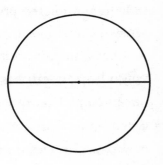

A World Cup in Viareggio

If I close my eyes and try to remember the month of June 2002, if I think once again about my World Cup, the first thing I feel is disbelief. Did I really spend forty-one days in Japan? Did I really referee Brazil-Germany, in the World Cup final? When I remember these things, I'm overcome by a peculiar sense of unreality. Perhaps it's that the experience, the entire World Cup period, was so beautiful and so perfect that sometimes I think I might just have dreamed it. It was a dream that lasted more than a month. Fortunately there are videos and newspaper articles that testify to events. And had I been able to write a script for those weeks beforehand, I wouldn't have made the slightest change to what actually happened – the final included.

Actually, there is one thing I would have changed: the location. I would have filmed my World Cup in Viareggio, perhaps with a few scenes from Lucca and the surrounding area. Had I been the director I would never have put 13,000 kilometres between me and my family.

A new starting point

But though I was just an actor in that film, despite directing the final, I can't deny that the 2002 World Cup represented an important stage in my life, both as a referee and as a man. However, I'd rather not speak about it as my own personal final. Personal finals involve pauses, rest, reflection – final reckonings – and I'm not ready for anything like that yet. People say that on reaching such a peak the best thing to do is to quit, to 'get out while the going's good'. That way everyone remembers you as you were at your height, but you don't run the risk of ruining your reputation with later mistakes. But I like what I do too much. I look upon my experience in Japan over the summer of 2002 as a new starting point, from which I can set off again. I hope it is an intermediate point along a journey that will last a good while longer. Indeed, the hundreds of emails I received encouraging me to continue, following the rumours that after the World Cup I was going to stop refereeing, were for me a real confidence boost.

I'm forty-three years old and I still have some years ahead of me as a referee. In the years to come I'd simply like to do what I've done so far, with the same motivation, the same passion and the same concentration.

I'm convinced that if I were to decide I'd achieved something, or I'd gone as far as I could go, then I'd probably end up on an unstoppable downward slide. If you persuade yourself that you're owed something, you start to think you can do things without having to commit yourself, without having to apply yourself as you used to. But it doesn't work like that.

My last World Cup

Naturally, it would be foolish of me to undervalue, or to pretend to undervalue, a World Cup final, if for no other reason than so few of them have been played – just think, only sixteen from 1930 to the present day. To be one of the small number of referees who have been in charge of one is certainly something extraordinary, perhaps even a little piece of history (assuming that history can ever really be concerned in any way with football). Whatever, for a referee's own personal results table, it is the most one can ever aspire to.

Having said that, I'm sure that the day when I feel I've really arrived will be the day when I'll stop refereeing. The day when I realize I no longer have the commitment I once had, when I feel weariness at the thought of training, or when I delude myself into thinking I can afford to give up work and my daily commitments, that'll be the day when I'll hang up my whistle.

For the moment my aim is to referee for as long as the current rules allow me, which is until I'm forty-five. When the next World Cup comes around in Germany I'll be forty-six, so it is a mathematical certainty that my World Cup experience finished with the Japan and Korea tournament. To put this in writing leaves something of a bitter taste in my mouth. I would love to set out for a new World Cup, with even more enthusiasm than I had for the one I've just been involved in, but these are the rules of the game.

But let's play the 'if' game again, and pretend that I'm the screenwriter of my life and my career. In that case I'd rather the rules were different. I think it would be better if a referee's participation in an event like the World Cup depended not on his date of birth, but on his performance. Some footballers have had particularly long careers and have achieved great things: Dino Zoff won a World Cup at the age of forty, Gary McAllister of Liverpool won a UEFA Cup final at thirty-seven, and was man of the match. If a similar date of birth 'rule' had been applied to them, they wouldn't have been allowed to win at the 'wrong' age. I think things might, and should, work like this for a referee as well. He ought to be the one to judge whether he has the motivation and ability to continue and, if he has, then it ought to be his physical and technical performance on which the decision rests. To reject the services of experienced, skilled referees just because they are forty-five years of age is a real pity for football, a waste of resources that have been preciously built up over the years. But I'm a referee, not a screenwriter.

From the World Cup to the Italian Cup

My next match after the World Cup final was in the first round of the Italian Cup, which involves teams from Serie B and Serie C. The day before, a friend asked me what it was like to go from Brazil–Germany to Sampdoria–Siena, the game I was to referee. I answered with what might sound like a cliché, but it's the honest truth: 'It doesn't matter what the game is, I want to be the best at what I do.' It would be really annoying if anyone even imagined that I refereed a match badly because I was lacking in enthusiasm, lacking concentration or that I hadn't worked sufficiently on my preparation. Of course, there are times when your performance isn't superlative even though you've done the best you can in terms of preparation. You feel bad about that, but you know it hasn't been down to you.

Lack of preparation, on the other hand, is all down to you – and I can't bear the idea of creating a bad impression.

So, even though I was physically a bit out of shape, even though my season had ended on 30 June and the new one was beginning early, I set out to get ready as best I could for Sampdoria–Siena. I did this because I always approach life with the same attitude: I only enjoy something when I am fully committed to do my best.

Build-ups

Naturally I don't want to suggest that a World Cup final is in any way a match like any other. It's not like that for the players, it's not like that for the supporters; so it can't be like that for the person who is asked to referee it. This is a match that concludes a four-year 'season', a game during which you must concentrate every resource you have, because even subconsciously, it is more demanding.

All matches are worthy of maximum attention, but the one that ends a tournament involving the best national teams in the world requires your very best performance. You have to approach it with the conviction and the peace of mind that comes from having done everything in your power to be prepared for the event: a spectacle that is, of its kind, unique.

Peace of mind, I believe, is the only way to describe the build-up to any sporting event I'm called to take part in. For me, peace of mind comes from not only knowing that I've dedicated myself 100 per cent to careful preparation, but also knowing when to pull the plug and relax. I always manage to get a good night's sleep the night before an important game and perhaps even catch an hour or so in the afternoon before an evening match. I am lucky in this respect, and I do think it really is a matter of luck. I'm able to switch easily from total attention, from absolute concentration, to total relaxation. I think this is the only way to avoid stress levels going over the top, something which could put the game's result in jeopardy.

The ability to govern one's emotions like this has its down side – for example, it doesn't help you keep many memories. The day before the World Cup final is not exactly 'normal', but if you manage not to feel any special pressures or tensions, it's obvious that you'll remember fewer details; your mind retains fewer events when you're relaxed, even your own thoughts and other people's words fade away. All build-ups tend to be pretty much alike, and so they have all become somewhat mixed up in my mind. But if I had to choose between fewer memories and more peace of mind, I'd choose the latter every time.

Plan. But not too much

I started refereeing at the age of seventeen and yet my first match, my first professional match, my first in Serie A, my first international: none of these milestones were part of a 'plan'. I like planning goals for the future, but not in the very long term because I also love the changes, the sudden shifts, the new challenges that life puts in your way: the challenges that you cannot predict. I do not have long-term object-ives because I know that the siren call of change might just distract me from pursuing them with the right amount of con-viction. After all, although I'm not an astrology enthusiast,

I know that these features are typical of those, like me, who are born under the sign of Aquarius.

Of course, when I first became involved in refereeing at a high level I never set myself the target of directing a World Cup final. This is because it was something that didn't depend exclusively on my own ability or my own application: you can't set yourself a goal that doesn't depend on your own talent and effort.

Just a few days before setting off for Japan, I was asked, 'What do you want to get out of this World Cup?' I replied that a referee should never want to get anything out of a tournament, because his job doesn't allow him to want to get anything. The referee's role means that he has to do what he is required to do, i.e. to referee a match. Whether it's the first or the last of the tournament, he has to be ready and has to provide the best performance that he is capable of giving. There then follows a series of factors that are outside your control, factors that can determine whether you referee any more than a couple of matches, or even perhaps the final.

But it doesn't just depend on you. Obviously you have to perform well, but you can't do any more than that. Sometimes it's enough, but only if your good performances are helped along by something else – specifically the elimination of your own country's team. You might perform extremely well, but if your country's team also does well then, despite your best efforts, you find yourself 'knocked out'; something I experienced in the World Cup in France in 1998 and again in the European Championships in 2000.

The 1998 World Cup and Euro 2000

At the time of the World Cup in France, despite being fortunate enough to be very well regarded, I was still considered a 'young' referee, especially compared to my colleagues. Referees such as Mario van der Ende, Marc Batta, Kim Milton Nielsen, Josè Maria Garcia Aranda and Hugh Dallas all had much greater international experience than I did. For some this was because they were older than me, for others it was because some northern European countries promote referees to international matches much earlier than in Italy. Kim Milton Nielsen, for example, just a few months younger than me, became an international referee at twenty-eight, something unimaginable in my country.

First of all I was given the job of refereeing Holland–Belgium – effectively a derby – a delicate and demanding match, and following that, France–Denmark. Then Italy went through to the quarter-finals and at that stage all the referees whose countries were still in the competition were taken off the roster.

By Euro 2000 I was a member of the top group of referees and was appointed to Holland–Czech Republic, then to a difficult match, not least from the security point of view, between England and Germany, and then to the quarter final between France and Spain. But when Italy qualified for the semi-final, I obviously couldn't be selected. Although everyone knew this rule right from the beginning, I remember the disappointment when my early return home became a certainty. As they say, hope is always the last thing to die. But seeing my neighbour, the French referee Marc Batta, prepare his bags even before the official announcement made me feel very sad. In part this was eased by the fact that I knew I'd done a good job and that my not staying was not the consequence of my performance, but of the results of the Italian national team.

If Italy had qualified for the later stages in Japan–Korea, I would have had to bow out well before the last match. It's precisely for this reason that I think it's wrong for a referee to set himself career goals, especially for a referee lucky enough to come from a nation whose team is among the best in the world and normally reaches the final stages of important tournaments. And I say lucky enough without any hint of irony. Emotionally I feel strongly about any event my country is involved in and I really do feel proud every time Italy wins anything – in any field.

Despite the disappointment of my early exit in both France and Belgium, it did give me an opportunity to enjoy something that is very dear to me, but for obvious reasons I rarely get to experience – the atmosphere and emotion of being in a crowd, being part of the sense of festival that only football can bring. I remember the great streams of people of various nationalities who flowed happily and harmoniously down the Champs Elysées and the wonderful choreography of the French and Spanish supporters all mixed together in the main square in Bruges. In Paris, once I'd been 'knocked out', I decided to stay on with my wife to see France–Italy in the quarter-finals: what drama, what colours, and what a disappointment when Italy lost.

I watched the final of Italia '90, again with my wife, when I was still refereeing in Serie C. Thinking back to that day, the first thing that I remember is the Olympic Stadium in a fantastic state, full to capacity not only with supporters from Germany and Argentina, the finalists, but with fans from all over the world.

It was a truly wonderful feast of football. And I don't mean that from a purely sporting point of view. It was more about the interaction and sense of community between the fans, all of them different in terms of culture and experience yet united by their love of football. There was just one blemish on this perfect evening. During the Argentine national anthem many of the crowd began to whistle and jeer – something that can be put down to the supporters' passion, and a sort of revenge for Italy having been knocked out by the South Americans.

An uphill start

In Japan and Korea, the absence of large numbers of many nations' fans had a direct influence on the football of many teams and consequently on the World Cup as a whole. The tournament was a great success, but it was more media-based, more televisual. Yes, there were some 'away' supporters for the national teams – English and Irish, for example – but the vast majority of those in the stadiums were Japanese and Korean. Because of this there was less of the atmosphere that is inspired by the meeting of peoples, customs and cultures – something that I think is every bit as important as the competition itself.

But let's take a step back and look through my World Cup experience in chronological order. When I think about it, I realize that it didn't get off to a very good start. The official confirmation that I would be there reached me early in 2002, after the final meeting of FIFA's Referees' Panel. It wasn't a surprise. I can't deny that I had been expecting it: in some ways I'd been banking on it.

What was a surprise to the entire Italian camp, however, was that none of our assistants were selected, something that had never happened before in any of the big football tournaments. And here it is also worth remembering that the Italian camp has always enjoyed a first-rate tradition and status. We made no protest or complaint; it would have been very serious indeed if we had been among the first to show disrespect for the rules. But there was some bitterness, especially from a personal perspective, because among those assistants who were most likely to be selected for the World Cup were many good colleagues who I had spent many an hour training with and with whom I had refereed many games. The presence of an Italian assistant at the World Cup would have been the right kind of recognition for a national group that has historically performed at the highest level and which is now working well to cope with a difficult job.

At the end of March 2002 I was called to Seoul for a training course, together with all the referees and assistants who had been selected for the tournament finals – some seventy people in total. There was to be a theoretical part, consisting of an analysis and discussion on the FIFA directives regarding various technical matters, and then a physical check-up and fitness test for each of us. On arriving in Seoul, I was feeling under the weather, which I initially put down to jetlag or just tiredness from the journey. But the following morning I woke up with a temperature which got decidedly worse as the day wore on. It quickly turned into a raging fever that kept me in bed for almost the entire course. I really was feeling down, especially because this course was an important moment in preparing for the World Cup. The long hours spent watching the television in my room simply aggravated my depression. This wasn't so much because of the sumo wrestling matches that were broadcast almost continuously by the local station, to the extent where I became quite an expert, but rather because of the terrible programmes offered by Italy's RAI International – a real invitation to commit suicide. But, joking apart, what really put me out were certain nasty and alarmist comments following my forced withdrawal from the physical tests: as though a referee weren't allowed to come down with a bout of flu.

Something that's normal for an athlete seems not to be normal for a referee, not even for a referee who, like me, has two young daughters and who is therefore open to the risk of picking up all the bugs they bring home from school. Fortunately just a month or so previously I had undergone the same athletic tests for UEFA, and the Referees' Panel decided they counted.

Kick-off

It was an uphill start, but from then onwards everything began to improve. My first match was Argentina–England, one of the games that as soon as the groups had been announced in Busan in December 2001 I had really wanted to referee. Out of superstition I had avoided even trying to find out whether it was going to be in Korea or Japan and exactly when it was to be played. I can't pretend that the news, which reached me when I was in Korea on 24 May, didn't fill me with an intense feeling of satisfaction.

I've already said that all matches are equal . . . well, some are more equal than others. The interest in and importance of this one was clear to everyone – this was a game that went beyond football.

To have such an important match entrusted to me confirmed how I was considered within the game and this was something of which I was very proud. However, I immediately had the feeling that, as with all things in life, there was another side to the coin – something far less gratifying and certainly more worrying – the element of risk. To start the World Cup with such an important, demanding match, under the spotlights of the entire world, might also present a problem – if it were to go badly then my World Cup might well be seriously compromised. Wouldn't it have been better to start off with a quieter match, with a greater chance of everything running smoothly?

But faced with a choice between challenge and fear, I never have any doubts: I'll take the challenge every time.

Argentina–England has history: Diego Maradona's infamous handballed goal he dubbed *mano di dios* (Hand of God); David Beckham's sending off and all the subsequent fuss it caused; not to mention the history of war between the two countries over the Falklands/Malvinas. Despite these things, all things considered, it went more than well, and I say this despite the fact that I'm usually highly critical of my own performance. In this case, however, I was immediately aware that I'd refereed a good match, one of those where you manage to relay certain messages to the players that they manage to transform into correct, disciplined behaviour.

News of my being appointed to Argentina–England reached me on 24 May. The Referees' Panel published the list of the first thirty-six games allocated to the thirty-six referees. Some hours before the official announcement rumours had been going round that my name had been seen alongside the match on a TV graphic that had been put up by mistake and was then immediately removed. But I was faithful to my old habit of celebrating, even to myself, only on receiving confir-

mation. After the list was published there was a press con
ference and we referees were given permission to speak to
the journalists: something that happened only three times
throughout the entire tournament.

The vast majority of the journalists asked to speak to me;
further proof if any was needed of the importance of the
match. But two weeks were to pass from that day until
Argentina and England met on the pitch. There was still plenty
of time to get ready for the game, which was to take place in
Sapporo, in the north of Japan, where the weather was cool
and damp, a change from the warm, sunny climate we were
then enjoying in our base near Tokyo.

One part of preparing to referee, apart from training and
developing concentration, is to watch a match. There were
three stadiums near Tokyo – Yokohama, Ibaraki and Saitama
– all just a few hours' coach ride away. Two matches involved
Argentina and England and at least one of them was within
easy reach for me, but I chose instead not to go and see either
of them. Perhaps this was to avoid developing a preference
for one team over another; perhaps so I could watch both
matches live on TV and start getting ready, right from the very
beginning, for my turn.

Study more, referee better

For a referee an essential part of getting ready for a match is to do some research. The first thing I try to memorize when I study a game on television is how the teams play, the tactics they use on the pitch, both for defending and attacking. It's important to understand how their games progress, how the various moves are played out, to observe how they deal with their set pieces, their free kicks and corners. I then move on to an analysis of individuals, because carrying out a game plan depends on the characteristics of the various players. To put it simply, I'm convinced that the more you study then the easier your task as a referee becomes.

Obviously watching a match live isn't enough, so a video recording becomes essential, as it lets you see all the moves repeatedly, allowing you to focus attention on the most important moments in the game. Research requires time and commitment, but it pays dividends in the long run.

Indeed, I'm convinced that study and research are essential in any activity. An apparently trivial, but perfectly clear example of this is when research helped me not being taken in by *Scherzi a parte*, an Italian television show in which famous people are the target of various tricks and jokes.

A company got in touch with me to propose an advertising endorsement for a supposed Internet Service Provider and invited me to a meeting in a Viareggio hotel. I made some enquiries about the company and discovered it was a real one, but also obtained some information which didn't quite match up with the things I was told by the people I eventually met. This set alarm bells ringing for me and so the joke was a flop.

The moral of the story is that if I hadn't done that simple research work, I would have fallen into the trap.

This need for knowledge is why I try to have at least one training session in the stadium in which I'm going to referee the following day – especially if I've never been there before. I did this for Argentina–England, which was to take place in a very special stadium, a completely covered dome, with the highly futuristic feature of a playing surface that, when not in use, is moved out of the dome and is 'parked' in the open air so the grass is allowed to breathe and grow. The pitch is brought back under cover only on the day before the match.

Training in the Sapporo dome, a ground that isn't particularly big (its capacity is about 40,000) with architecture that's more like a sports complex than an Italian football stadium, was very important for me. Only in this way did I manage to get to know the new surroundings, the different smells and sounds, so as to avoid being taken by surprise during the game itself and suffering the effects of disorientation.

A home match

Despite the fact I was refereeing in Japan, the game was almost like being 'at home', because in both teams there were players I'd refereed many times in the past. This was not just confined to the Argentinians who play in the Italian league, but also included many of the English players whom I'd often met in European, international and club competitions too. There was no danger of language problems as I speak Spanish and English, and with many of the Argentinians I could speak Italian quite happily. In fact, in this case too, knowledge helped – reciprocal knowledge – because this logic also works to the players' advantage. It gives them peace of mind and eliminates, or at least diminishes, any communication problems and, consequently, the possibility of error.

If you add respect and trust to language skills, the cocktail is perfect and it can give you the help you need to referee a good game. A player who knows you and appreciates you, for example, will tend to take any error of judgement you make on the pitch in his stride.

Knowledge can also help you get out of difficult situations, or situations that might put players and the referee into conflict. It might be by making a funny comment when you know there's no danger of being misunderstood. For example, during Argentina–England I remember that as we were going back onto the pitch after half-time Gabriel Batistuta was complaining about having been booked after just twelve minutes. Clearly it wouldn't have been a good idea for me to go into the reasons for my decision, but, knowing Batistuta well, I opted for a joke that might calm him down. The booking had been called for by my Canadian assistant and I said to the Argentinian forward: 'Of course you know the real reason why the assistant had you booked?' He looked at me and I added, 'He is Canadian, but he's originally from Chile!' joking on the rivalry between Chileans and Argentinians. Batistuta replied, 'Ah, so that's why!' He understood the joke, accepted the rules of the game, and the discussion ended there.

This series of circumstances worked in such a way as to make Argentina–England a good match, free from problems or any post-match tensions, even though for one of the two teams, Argentina, who lost, it was a serious blow to their prospects for qualifying.

With this testament to the virtues of knowledge and study I don't in any way intend to suggest that without it things are necessarily destined to work out badly, but I do think it's a good guideline in life to try and minimize the element of luck involved in doing the best you can.

The World Cup continues

My second match, which followed games as fourth official for Germany–Cameroon and Belgium–Russia, was for the knockout stage between Japan and Turkey. I'd seen Japan–Russia and Japan–Belgium at the grounds and the thing that had struck me most of all had been the enthusiastic involvement of the home crowd, a crowd that perhaps didn't know all that much about football, but were extraordinarily communicative and generous, keen to get to know the world of football at first hand.

I felt I was in good physical shape, thanks in part to the help of the two Belgian trainers who were in charge of the referees' preparation, and despite the fact that the match was played under constant rain, the ground was in perfect condition thanks to an extremely efficient drainage system. Add to this the superstitions that link me to the Turkish team – it appears that the Turkish side has never lost a match I've refereed and so they look upon me as a good-luck charm – and everything was set for a good match.

And indeed this too turned out to be a positive, successful game.

My clearest memory, my lasting impression of the game, comes from the moment immediately after the final whistle. Following two hours of deafening support, as incessant as the rain, from the 40,000 excited Japanese supporters, there were ten seconds of absolute, total silence.

Their team had lost and their World Cup had come to an end. To me, those ten seconds seemed like an eternity. I understood now what is meant by a 'deafening silence'. Then – resounding and moving – came a long applause. The dream of the Japanese national team had come to an end, but with that applause the crowd sought to emphasize its gratitude for a result that they thought was excellent nonetheless. It was a magic moment, something I'd rarely experienced before. On the pitch many of the Japanese players were in tears while the Turkish side celebrated and it was a natural gesture for me to go over to the Japanese captain, Miyamoto, and say to him simply, 'I really think you should be proud of what you've done. Not sad. Proud.'

Pride in defeat

Those players, that team, had achieved more than had been asked of them before the World Cup. To have reached the last sixteen and to have lost with great dignity represented a thoroughly respectable result for a team who were considered outsiders for the tournament. In speaking to the Japanese captain in that way, and at such a delicate moment after what was undoubtedly a painful defeat, I sought to express my own deep feelings and to give credit to those who had lost after having given everything in the attempt to win. I believe that in today's world, and here I'm thinking not only of the world of professional sport, we have lost sight of the value of an honourable defeat. Something that ought to be an excep tional circumstance, i.e. triumph, has ended up becoming the norm, the minimum objective. Let's be clear about this,

I am not an intransigent follower of de Coubertain, I don't believe that any sportsman should derive the most pleasure from, or set himself the ultimate goal of, simply participating in an event. Simply taking part isn't enough for me, I like to try to win. And I try to do so in every way possible, obviously as long as the means are legitimate. But in trying to win there is also the knowledge that one might come second, or third . . . or last.

The 'abnormal' competitor isn't the loser, the 'abnormal' is the winner, the one who does something different, something better than all the others, and as such deserves to be celebrated. But it does not follow that all the others are consequently failures. The culture of triumph at all costs, of competition taken to its limits, inevitably leads to the use of unfair, even illegal means and ends up with the possible use of methods that rely on deceit, on abuse of power, even on doping. These are the antithesis of the values that are the foundations of sport and the cornerstones of civil society. I don't think this reasoning can be misunderstood as an unreal, utopian point of view, nor for that of an incurable optimist – two categories to which I really don't belong – but I remain convinced that total respect is due to those who lose while trying to win, but find themselves up against a better opponent, better at least on that particular day. It is not fair to judge by results alone, the efforts made in achieving those results must also be taken into consideration.

This is what I wanted to tell the Japanese captain – they had sought victory, but had been beaten by a team that had played better. And his smile confirmed that my English and his English were somehow similar. The infinite applause of the supporters gave me the impression that our idea of what a sporting event should be was in some way a shared one.

Some similar events might include the third- and fourth-place final in Korea between Korea and Turkey, which ended with much embracing between the winning and losing players, or the great applause offered as a tribute by the supporters of Leicester City when their team was relegated to the First Division. These things make me think that the idea of football as an opportunity for healthy sporting challenge, rather than as a war to the death, is not just a memory for a few idealists who find themselves labelled old-fashioned. I'll never forget the crowd at Old Trafford in Manchester during a Champions' League match when the Red Devils were three goals down to Real Madrid. There was no whistling, no booing, just encouragement for the team and at the end, despite the 2–3 result, a long, grateful applause.

A consideration of the culture of sport would involve a very long discussion indeed, because for Italy this would mean dealing with the school system, the lack of sporting facilities and the lack of mass participation at childhood and youth level.

Some sort of foundation activity is essential to help shape the right attitude of those who in the future will become essentially 'passive' sportsmen or women – just simple enthusiasts. In the same way family support is necessary, real support from parents who all too often tend to exaggerate the importance of competitiveness and of success at all costs for their children.

I don't want in any way to demonize parents, I know that letting youngsters participate in sport often involves sacrifices in money, time and energy, and not everyone can afford these. But no one should ever lose sight of the real values that lie at the heart of sport. An honourable defeat is hard and enervating, but there's a value in it that makes it worth accepting. It's a value worth cultivating.

And this is how I explain the words I offered to Miyamoto following Japan–Turkey, or even my spur-of-the-moment gesture of lifting Samuel Kuffour up from the pitch after the Bayern Munich player had just suffered defeat against Manchester United in the last seconds of the 1999 Champions' League final in Barcelona.

Referees don't celebrate

If I had to choose an image to promote the culture of sport, I would choose the things I saw after the Turkey–Korea match, with the Turkish players joining their just defeated opponents in a lap of honour to celebrate what was a success for them both – simply to have reached the third-place final of the World Cup. And then, just as they were about to climb up on to the podium for the prize-giving, some of the players, such as Bulent Korkmaz and Abdullah Ercan, had their children come over and they carried them on their shoulders – truly an extraordinary sight. It was such a wonderful scene that I can't deny I even felt a bit envious of those who were allowed to share such joy publicly, and with their nearest and dearest.

But because of his role the referee, as we all know, is not allowed to celebrate. Having said this, however, immediately after my World Cup final, my 'team' was granted some recognition which might have appeared very small, but for me had great symbolic value. FIFA protocol is extremely strict with regard to ceremonial matters immediately after matches; we had been told the day before the game that we would be called up on to the podium set up on the pitch and that Sepp Blatter, FIFA President, would then hand us the medals that are given to the referee and his assistants. We were then to clear the podium to make way for the players.

And we were ready to do just this, but a surprise came once we were actually up there. The speaker introduced us and the crowd responded with an ovation. For us it was a great feeling and for President Blatter it was the cue to bend protocol: instead of handing us the medals, he put them around our necks. It might seem like a small gesture, but for us it meant a lot, granting both solemnity and spontaneity to the ceremony. But the surprise, which at one stage meant I fell down one of the steps, wasn't over: Blatter had us all line up, just like we were players, to receive further applause from the crowd, our medals hanging from our necks, photographers and cameramen recording the scene.

It was recognition for us there on the pitch, but indirectly it was also recognition for referees everywhere who saw their role being presented in a positive light. It was truly an extraordinarily emotional moment that would have been perfect for me had I been able to share it with my family. But there was a way of showing my family how close I felt to them even though they were some 13,000 kilometres away. I quickly kissed the finger of my left hand, where I wear my wedding ring. This was enough to let them all know that in my moment of great joy I was thinking of my loved ones.

I'd like to take a few words to discuss the unwritten rule that prevents the referee and his team of assistants from celebrating a good job well done. I remember the fuss that followed a celebratory gesture, quite a mild one, made by an Italian referee at the end of a match that was obviously particularly important to him and which he felt he'd refereed well. I don't agree with the criticism he received: it was a spontaneous, natural gesture. It's obvious that we are required to demonstrate respect for the role we play on the pitch, that any display of uncalled for jubilation would not only be lacking in style but would be wrong. The figure of the referee, however, has to be comparable to that of the sportsman. If the performance required of us is closer to that of the athlete than that of the gowned judge, free from emotion, then it's perfectly understandable if there are reactions similar to those of a sportsman – including expressing joy at a job well done. I'm not suggesting taking off and waving the black shirt then running to embrace the fourth official, but why be outraged or surprised? If I live during the week just as a professional player does – training, going off to camp – then isn't it only natural that I will gradually acquire similar behaviour and reactions of those who play? More understanding for referees' 'outbursts' would make it easier for the players themselves to feel more on the same wavelength, more 'on the same side' as those who, like them, have to try to give their best in acting out, albeit with different roles, the same show.

'A different way of taking part in sport' was a slogan used some years ago in a campaign for the recruitment of new referees. Today, certainly as far as referees at the professional level are concerned, that way is perhaps a little less different.

Flashbacks of the final

I've already written about my World Cup final in Japan at length, but of course there are many more details, images and memories of that magical evening, an evening which, as I've already mentioned, is destined to remain a one-off in my career. I'll try to illustrate them all by means of a flashback that I think is important.

It was a minor incident, certainly marginal from a purely footballing point of view, but it allows me to explain a way of interpreting a match that is crucial for a referee.

It was Edmilson's back-to-front shirt incident.

It's right in the middle of the final and I notice that a Brazilian player's shirt is ripped so I ask him to change it. He receives a new one from the touchline, takes off the torn one and then starts a strange dance as his arms flail in his attempts to put it on. He ties himself in knots while battling with the shirt. One attempt, two attempts, but no joy. The shirt just won't cooperate, despite some team-mates now trying to help. Then a collective 'Ooh!' of relief from the crowd turns into general laughter: he's got the shirt on, but it's back-to-front. Eventually he gets it the right way round and the stadium erupts in applause to mark the player's victory, just like he'd scored from a spectacular overhead kick and so the final can now continue.

I mention this not just as a memory of an amusing little incident, but also to illustrate a slightly more serious issue. If I'd applied the rules to the letter, Edmilson would have had to leave the pitch, only to be allowed back on once he was dressed properly. Asking him to leave would have meant penalizing his team. But penalizing a World Cup final team for a change of shirt would have meant a failure on my part in interpreting the attitude of that game; it would have been a betrayal of the spirit of fair play that both teams were displaying on the pitch. It was far better to waste some time – even though I hadn't reckoned on a change of shirt being transformed into a contortionist exhibition – than jeopardize the good atmosphere with a strict application of the rules.

Two

Preparation

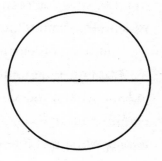

Run, referee, run

Preparation is the key to understanding the way I look at the 'refereeing trade'. In order to referee a game of football well, you have to be aware of what you have been asked to do and to make sure you're in the best condition for doing it – all of which takes commitment, work and attention.

It means not leaving anything to chance.

Training is automatically associated with running and, indeed, what a referee does for ninety minutes on a football pitch is run. In today's game, which is played at a very high tempo, with great intensity and an often exaggerated sense of competition, a referee has to be able to count on an athleticism that is equal to the speed of what happens around him, and be in a condition to make the best possible decision.

To realize how much faster today's football is played, just watch a match from fifteen to twenty years ago. At first it looks like the video isn't working properly – all the players seem to be running in slow motion – but, of course, that's not the problem. Rather it's today's players who do everything so much quicker, sometimes so quickly that they don't have time to think about what they're doing. They are simply repeating movements that they've practised an infinite number of times in training, in fact their speed is such that sometimes they don't even have enough time to lift their heads before passing the ball. This has reached the point where, in recent years, much greater attention has been paid not only to the colour of the players' shirts, but also to the colour of socks and shorts, because they're useful for distinguishing team-mates from opponents. As a consequence, in an attempt to avoid further problems, referees have been asked to use coloured socks instead of the previously ubiquitous black ones.

The referee has to be aware that the most hazardous stage for him during a match is towards the end, when, due to tiredness, players tend to make more mistakes – bad passes, miscontrolling the ball, taking too many touches and so on. This increases the likelihood of them committing fouls, infringing the rules and can lead to dangerous situations. This means that the referee has to be even more careful in the final stages of a game and must be in an ideal psychological and physical condition to make tough decisions in difficult situations.

Obviously after running for the entire game, the referee is more tired than he was at the beginning, but twenty minutes from the whistle the referee can't raise his arm, turn towards the bench and ask to be substituted. His training therefore has to take this into account and has to allow him to remain rational and together, even in the last seconds of a game. It's at this stage where he might have to make difficult decisions that are now even more critical because there is so little time left in the game - particularly if a last-gasp goal means that a team has no chance of coming back.

Since no one has yet invented a pill for achieving this condition, it is vitally important to dedicate hours during the week to training and exercise on the pitch. As a referee I can now say that I've enjoyed quite a long working life. I've been working for over twenty-five years and I think I'm a reliable witness to the changes that have taken place in athletic training during that period.

When I first started refereeing, and right up until I reached the international level, there was much less attention paid to physical preparation – probably because football in those days didn't really call for any special athletic preparation for referees. A bit of training here and there, less frequent and less intense than today's, was enough to prepare for adequate performance on a Sunday. Back then training a couple of times a week was the norm and if you missed a session because of the weather or some other hiccup, that wasn't a problem.

Things aren't like that now, so much so that I normally advise youngsters who are just starting out to train as much as possible from the very beginning because they'll feel the benefit of tough, demanding, continuous athletic training when they are a few years older. By then they'll be able to bank on the reserves accumulated by getting their body used to a certain pace of training.

It's much more difficult, and much less effective, to teach your body how to train when you're older.

To show the amount of attention paid to physical fitness

today, it's useful to look at the methods of evaluation that are used. Let's take one of the tests used worldwide to judge a referee's state of fitness: the Cooper Test. This is a test in which you are required, among other things, to run a predetermined minimum distance in twelve minutes. Over the course of the last ten to fifteen years this minimum distance has increased from the 2,400 metres required at the 1990 World Cup in Italy, to today's 2,700 metres. At the tests for the last World Cup the average distance covered by a referee was a little over 3,000 metres – considerably more than the minimum. And up until ten years ago there were very few who ever managed to reach 2,700 metres. If you think that seems easy, just try running 3,000 metres in under twelve minutes. Obviously professional middle-distance runners are exempt from the test.

The same applies to the speed tests over fifty metres (to be covered in seven and half seconds) and 200 metres (thirty-two seconds), both of which were easily passed by all the referees – so much so in fact that a change in evaluation procedures is now being considered. What's needed are new tests that provide better analysis of referees' fitness and are more in line with the features of today's football.

Recently, in many countries, including Italy, the so-called 'yo-yo' test has been introduced, which is a series of sprints – twenty metres forwards, twenty metres backwards –with a break of ten seconds between each sprint. The initial speed is set by a beep that indicates the moment by when each distance of twenty metres has to be covered. This speed then increases until you reach the line after the beep and you're eliminated. It's a test of maximum performance and helps evaluate the individual's athletic condition.

From the medical point of view, today's tests are also much more thorough: heart, blood, muscles, constitution, from heart rate to weight, from lactic acid production to stress recovery times, all of these are regularly checked and evaluated.

There are tests, but there is also instruction on methodology. The training programmes that were once left to chance, or to an individual's initiative, are nowadays defined by athletic coaches who use avant-garde methods and varied workloads over the course of the year in order to obtain good results on the pitch.

For over ten years now the AIA (Associazione Italiana Arbitri), the Italian Referees' Association, has run a network of training centres spread throughout the country which organize specific training sessions for referees and assistants working in Serie A and B, as well as at the lower levels.

Training in each of these centres is run by a coach and co-ordinated by a director at the headquarters. Over the course of the season he makes sure that the work-load is the same for everyone and periodically checks up on progress, thereby maintaining a unified programme that meets the various demands that present themselves during the championship.

The critical points in our training and evaluation are the placements we attend at Coverciano, where the football Federation's Technical Centre is based. These placements involve physical tests that are carried out during the season, together with two training sessions with different workloads depending on whether or not each referee has to work in a match over the weekend. Summer training also receives special attention. Every year since 1991 the referees and assistants of Serie A and B have gone on a twelve-day camp to Sportilia in the Tuscan–Romagna mountains.

FIFA and UEFA have recently adopted similar methods with the creation of an ad hoc framework for physical preparation, run by Professor Werner Helsen. Thanks to this arrangement the referees of the Federation, who have fewer chances to engage in such detailed programmed training, receive a weekly personalized schedule via email.

Werner Helsen was a player in the Belgian top division and went on to work as a trainer in the second division while at the same time becoming a teacher of motorial science at the University of Louvain. Before Euro 2000 he was asked by UEFA to oversee the referees' training during the tournament and the results were so positive that his position was confirmed for the 2002 World Cup.

Given that the referees and assistants all came from such diverse places, from the month of March 2002, immediately after we had all taken part in the first preparatory workshop, Professor Helsen sent us each a detailed weekly training programme. The twofold aim of this was to help get us ready for matches in the various national championships and, of course, for the World Cup.

The training sessions were recorded on a heart-rate monitor and each week the data from the sessions was downloaded onto a computer and emailed to FIFA. In this way, although spread out all over the world and thousands of kilometres apart, each of our training sessions was checked and monitored.

Once the tournament was under way we each received tailor-made training with different levels of intensity depending on the time available between matches. The benefits of this careful physical training were clear to see – not only did the tests produce excellent results, but there were no muscular injuries at all.

To feel physically fit throughout a tournament that lasts forty days and which comes, for we Europeans, at the end of a very demanding season, isn't easy. If we managed to achieve this, then it was certainly all down to the methods used.

I remain convinced, however, that as with players, the best referee trainer is the referee himself. It is essential to know oneself and, away from the communal programmes and objectives, each individual has to know when to accelerate and when to slow down. The human body is not a machine that always runs at the same levels of performance; so what's required is to develop an ability to evaluate oneself.

If physical training is essential at the highest levels, then I'm convinced it's also valuable at the lower levels, where it establishes a foundation for development and, as I've mentioned, is an investment for the future. I'm sure that if I'd had the opportunities that exist today when I was starting out, it would all be less of an effort than it is for me today.

Another little tip that I'd like to give to those starting out is to try and train when they're not tired. Obviously, if you work then it's not easy to train during the day. This means you end up going out onto the pitch when you're a bit tense, both physically and mentally, after knocking off from work. To engage in physical activity that generates further tiredness is not easy and this is the stage when you might be tempted to say, 'Well, I'll stop now. I quit here. I'm off.' There's much more benefit in trying to train at times of the day when you aren't too tired from work – in the early afternoon, for example, which indeed is the same time when you'd normally referee, or even at lunchtime, especially appropriate for those who might want to lose a few kilos.

Personally I don't like training alone, I find it very mentally tiring, and so it's essential for me to train with others.

During the season the training centres make it easy, but it's complicated organizing this for tournaments that start once the season's over and your training partners are already on holiday. At that point you have to find a 'friend' who might be prepared to sacrifice his well-deserved holidays to sweat a bit with you.

Recovery

Faced with such physical demands, the recovery stage is crucially important, both during and at the end of a tournament.

During the summer break, the worst mistake you can

make is to switch off completely, to interrupt your physical training for any considerable length of time.

It's essential instead to continue doing something as an alternative to running – swimming for example, or cycling. Swimming really is just an example because despite living in a seaside town, I don't really love the water. But to swim or not to swim, the important thing is to move. By doing this you rest joints that have been put under enough stress during the season – such as knees and ankles – while at the same time maintaining your muscular tone and aerobic capacity. This makes it easier and less tiring to start training again for the next season.

Even during the season it can be useful to do some different types of training, something different from running, for example 'aqua-jogging' – running in a swimming pool with a special jacket that helps you float.

Recovery is an integral part of any discussion of training, and this is especially true for someone who, like me, is no longer a youngster. It is worthwhile considering recovery both from a dietary perspective – for replacing energy and nutrients at a bodily level – and from the physical and psychological point of view. This might be achieved through a session with a physiotherapist or some type of specific training.

In particular, the help of a physiotherapist, the classic masseur, has an important role. In helping me recover quickly and avoid the development of problems with muscles and tendons, the hands of Marco Terzi, the masseur who looks after me, are irreplaceable.

One of the occasions when recovery is particularly important is after an international match, especially if it's midweek and is then followed by another match at the weekend. International matches are normally in the evening and the journey back to Italy the following day takes several hours on the plane and in the car. Sitting for this length of time means that leg muscles tend to stiffen more than they usually would and when you get home and start training again, the tiredness is still there.

In these cases I find it extremely useful to go to the hotel gym, if there is one, the morning after the match and do twenty minutes or so on the treadmill or an exercise bike. If it's logistically possible I go back to the pitch where I refereed and do half an hour of running or exercises, so as to relax my legs and the rest of my body. That way I'm less tense for the journey home and I'm in better shape for the next day when training resumes for the next league match.

Diet

Another aspect of training which requires attention is diet – or rather dietary awareness. No referee has to become a diet freak, but I'm convinced that the right diet, not only before and after a match, but during the week as well, is essential for those who have to perform like athletes.

Athletes, obviously, live like athletes . . .

Though I'm not a doctor, I think my practical experiences regarding dietary matters might be of some interest. The basic principle is that our bodies must be nourished in the right way. Just as a car requires the right type of petrol, our body, which is nothing more than a very advanced organic machine, needs to pay as much attention to using the right fuel. Even so, the revolution I've witnessed in recent years has been remarkable. Up until not so long ago the 'right' food was plain rice and grilled steaks, which today everyone agrees is the wrong diet, especially if eaten just before a match. Meat is among those foods that are digested more slowly and which don't provide the body with the necessary kinds of energy for attaining top physical performance.

An athlete's diet, or to be more specific that of a referee, has to include energy-producing substances – carbohy drates, proteins and fats – as well as vitamins, minerals and hydration – in essence, all of the elements that make up a well-balanced, wide-ranging diet. But on the details, it's best to pass the ball over to the specialist dieticians.

For my own part I can add some subjective examples, habits and a few idiosyncrasies. Unlike some referees who choose almost to starve themselves on the day of a match, if I don't eat beforehand I risk feeling unwell. Obviously I have to eat my meal at some sort of reasonable time, and if the match is at three in the afternoon, then I sit down to eat at around 11.15. Normally it's just a plate of pasta with a tomato-based sauce or even just with olive oil, followed by a slice of jam tart. This side of things is so important to me that when

I choose the hotel where I spend the night before a match I take into account that I'll be wanting to eat my main meal at a time that more or less corresponds to the other guests' breakfast.

If the match is in the evening, on the other hand, the meal I have about 12.30–12.45 has to be a bit bigger and as well as pasta I'll eat some fish or ham, and often about 5–5.30 in the afternoon I'll have a small snack.

Equally important is what you eat after the match, when you need to replace the energy that you've burned off over the ninety minutes, but without going over the top. I prefer fruit, which also helps me drink less and thus avoid feeling unpleasantly bloated with liquid. So my post-match supper begins with fruit, before my usual plate of pasta, something I'll never give up eating.

It can be useful at certain points during the year, such as the change of season or when the weather's particularly hot or humid, or in certain moments during training, to supplement your normal diet with vitamins or special products, to try and help your body recover better. It's important, however, to read carefully what's written on the labels so as to avoid risks. In any case the best advice is to always consult a sports doctor.

As you will undoubtedly have gathered, my love for pasta is something I share with all good Italians, and it would be difficult for me to abandon a full plate of penne or spaghetti. Indeed, I love pasta so much that I often grin and bear those poor imitations – a far cry from what we would call pasta – that are put in front of me in various parts of the world.

The 2002 World Cup initially seemed a bit of a risk pasta-wise, but the Japanese chef at our hotel in Kisarazu produced some exceptionally good pasta-based meals. After all, Italian pasta has nowadays become part of the routine of almost all European referees on match days, and Swedish, French, German and Spanish waiters and restaurateurs, when they recognize the referee and assistants' team at a table, know immediately that a good plate of pasta is what's required.

I have a real food phobia about chicken and all bird meat. Don't they say that you need a touch of madness to be a referee? Well, this is the proof. I can't bear the idea of eating an animal that has feathers. It's not a matter of the taste or any sort of animal rights beliefs, it's a psychological phobia – for years my mother had to 'trick' me, into thinking that the turkey cutlets she put in front of me were actually veal.

As you can see, I'm no gourmand. I don't look upon food as a ritual, I hate sitting at a table for any longer than is necessary and that's why I love buffets, because I'm free to decide how long I spend eating.

Sometimes, however, especially when there are international matches, my local hosts go to great lengths to display the utmost care and attention in their hospitality by organizing long, drawn-out suppers in restaurants, which for me become a real ordeal.

The first thing I ask is that I have to sit at the table for no longer than is strictly necessary.

Awareness

Training isn't just a matter of looking after one's body. Training is also knowing exactly what you're setting out to do. And given that referees work on the football pitch, knowing about the specifics of football is essential. The rules are the first thing you have to know about. As the referee's role is to govern respect for the rules by those who are playing, it's obvious that he has to be the first person to know them.

If knowledge of the rules was enough to referee in Serie A it would be easy for any referee to get there. The seventeen rules of football are not particularly complicated. The whole lot are contained in a fifty-six-page booklet. They are so simple that it wouldn't be a bad thing if everyone, not just referees, but players and supporters as well, knew them. It would certainly help everyone understand what happens on the pitch.

But if knowledge of the rules is essential, even more important is an understanding of the possible interpretations of those rules.

One of the most-used expressions during the workshops and the seminars that are organized for referees before big international tournaments and the Italian league championship is *be consistent*. Subjective interpretation of the rules is indeed a frequent issue, and the search for consistency with oneself and with others is a constant concern. We work on this intensely, so as to make sure that scenarios are interpreted in the same way by any individual referee during any single game, series of games or throughout a competition. This is not an easy objective to pursue because, for as long as subjectivity remains in the game, similar situations can be interpreted in many different ways. And of course if a referee in the course of one single game makes inconsistent decisions, the whole thing becomes even more serious.

What's involved here is the individual referees footballing culture and his mentality. Everything becomes less easy to govern when the referees are from different countries and continents, with varied experience and customs.

There are rules that leave the referee considerable room for interpretation. Let's consider rule eleven, the offside rule. Here there are objective guidelines regarding the position of a player on the pitch and whether or not he should be penalized. In order to be offside he must be 'nearer to his opponents' goal line than both the ball and the second last opponent', unless 'he is in his own half of the field of play', 'level with the second last opponent', or 'level with the last two opponents'. Furthermore the ball must be 'played by one of his team', unless it comes from a 'goal kick, or a throw-in, or a corner kick'. Up to this point everything's simple.

But in order for any of the above to constitute an infringement of the rules, there is the matter of whether or not, the player is 'in the opinion of the referee, involved in active play'. This is where the individual's interpretation becomes important and, as this judgement is subjective, this can lead to contrasting decisions. And the words, 'in the opinion of the referee' appear in another of the most important rules, number twelve, which relates to fouls and misconduct. Here, the opinion of the referee is integral in deciding whether an obvious goal-scoring opportunity has been prevented by means of a foul – an offence punishable with a red card.

Through videos and analysis of situations and discussions, we work towards reaching a common interpretative philosophy. The aim is quite clear: there shouldn't be English or Italian, Spanish or German refereeing, but rather one single way, a denominator that is common to everyone. Meeting up periodically with referees from other countries and discussing these things, comparing the various interpretations that you sometimes hear, is certainly the best way. Our placements at Coverciano help at a national level, though it's obvious that complete homogeneity is still far away.

In recent years, the so-called 'open market' has meant that players from throughout the world can play in various national leagues and, as a consequence, these domestic championships have less strongly defined characteristics – even though a player normally absorbs the mentality of the country he plays in, rather than changing the mentality of those who play with him.

You might say that a referee's main gift has to be that of knowing how to adapt to the requirements of the match. This implies not just knowledge of the rules, but also, and above all else, knowledge of the context in which he is asked to work. This improves as you get to know the game, particularly if you study lots of matches – refereed by yourself or by others – with the help of those who know more than you do: the technical experts. The current movement in Italy towards using professional trainers for referees is very important for gaining this type of experience. It's a way of making sure that the referee is part of the structure of the game and understands its technical and tactical aspects.

I'm not suggesting that a referee necessarily has to attend a course run by trainers, but I am certain that a referee who truly understands football is better than one who only knows, even to the point of perfection, the rules. There are already many local divisions that hold technical meetings which referees at the amateur level are required to attend.

For some years now the Italian national referees' commission for Serie A and B has been working with a federation coach, Roberto Clagluna, previously a coach for Lazio and Roma, and I believe his help has been invaluable. I think it's indispensable for a referee to know the tactics of the teams he's going to referee, the formations they use, because it's a very different thing refereeing a team that plays 4–4–2 than one that uses 3–4–3 or even 3–4–1–2. It's also important to know if the team uses the offside trap constantly, perhaps with a high defensive line, or whether they adopt an aggressive pressing game in midfield or in attack. It can be very useful, for example, for a referee to know that a team plays with a single attacker, a target-man, because his role will be to head the ball back to the midfielders, or to control it and hold the ball up, giving his team-mates time to come forward. Similarly it can be useful to know that a team play with three in defence, because the opponents will probably try to exploit the empty spaces on the wings to draw the defenders out, exposing the defence to attack from the midfielders.

These tactics affect the progress of the game and mean that the referee's attention will be directed towards some areas of the pitch more than others.

Some years ago the Italian team Foggia played three extremely fast attacking players and a goalkeeper who, as soon as he got the ball, could kick it long from his own area very accurately. A referee who wasn't prepared for this tactic, and didn't have the speed of a hundred-metre sprinter, would inevitably find himself at least fifty metres from the action, in the opposite penalty area, completely put out of the game by the keeper's long kick.

In recent times free kicks and corner kicks have become increasingly important, so no longer do referees leave anything to chance and real 'tactics' are used. The potential for fouls from set pieces is very high and so the referee has to try to predict how the movements of the players will shape up within the penalty area.

This is just an example, but there are many more that show how important a tactical analysis of the teams before the game is. This research is easy to carry out for Italian teams, as all the matches are broadcast on pay-per-view and can be recorded and studied. For international matches the job is a bit more difficult – especially for those teams whose league matches aren't broadcast in Italy – as the referee is only told of appointment some eight to ten days beforehand, which sometimes isn't enough to get hold of video footage.

Things are easier during tournaments, for example, during the 2002 World Cup the organizers– Jawoc in Japan and Kowoc in Korea – made sure that we all had videotapes of the games already played and if you happened to find your-self refereeing a team's second match but not their first, as happened to me, you could study the tape of the previous match and thus gain useful information from it.

Before each of my matches, and certainly before the final, I spent many hours watching these recordings. My method was simple: I took a blackboard, divided it into two sections and noted down in the two halves the features of each team that struck me most, so as to be able to memorize them better. I then passed them on to the other members of my team. Probable line-up, playing formation, main game-plans, technical characteristics, players' tactics – anything and every-thing that might help during a match.

Before the final, what had struck me most about Brazil was the ease with which the Brazilian defenders and midfielders changed roles and the way they had no fixed positions in their attacking play. As for the Germans, I concentrated on Bernd Schneider's role behind the forwards and the frequency with which Miroslav Klose headed down long balls from defenders playing them back to forward-running players. These things might seem obvious, but they do focus your attention on specific parts of the pitch. Japan and Turkey, on the other hand, shared a similarly aggressive midfield, with very quick players who were good at pressing and running at pace, which meant that the central area of the pitch was the one that demanded particular attention.

If you have a wide range of information available to you, you're better placed to be able to 'read' a game.

Reading: this term has to be fundamental to the referee, just as it is for managers. There is no type of refereeing that works well for all games. The referee has to develop an almost chameleon-like capacity to be able to adapt his own abilities to the requirements of the match. All matches are different and therefore they have to be dealt with in completely different ways. What has to prevail is a pragmatic style of refereeing, suitable for the type of match and for the particular moment within that match. Knowledge of the technical abilities of individual players, is of great importance. If a right-footed player is played on the left, then it's unlikely that he'll head for the goal line to cross, instead he'll naturally prefer to head for goal and shoot, so what happens in the penalty area becomes even more important.

If I know, for example, that David Beckham likes to kick the ball some fifty metres diagonally across the pitch with his right foot, then I know that the ball will most likely end up in a certain part of the pitch, so I move with this in mind and focus my attention on that area. If I know that a player is skilled in running down the wing and from there crossing into the box, I have to watch out for what's happening in the penalty area, where the ball will arrive: it's there, with the ball still far away, that difficult situations might well arise.

When I say these things to journalists, they almost always seem surprised because people don't normally imagine that a referee bothers to learn about the tactical and technical side of a team or an individual player. Instead they think all I worry about is a player's tendency or ability to dive. But this isn't what happens. I believe that knowledge helps to make the best possible decision, but I also want to make it clear that what I look for isn't knowledge of players' behaviour. I don't go onto the pitch with any bias; prejudices have no part to play in a referee's role. In Tuscany there's a saying that whoever gets scalded with boiling water ends up being afraid of cold water too. If I know that the water is boiling, then I'll try to avoid putting my hand under it – the more information I have regarding the temperature of that water, the less likely I'll be to scald my hand – but the referee has to try to see what happens and to evaluate it as he sees it, not to remember or to judge what has happened in the past.

In football, more than in other sports, physical contact between two opposing athletes is allowed, and can occur without this in any way constituting a violation of the rules. This is something that does not happen in sports such as basketball, for example, where contact is always judged to be foul play. But identifying a foul in football involves a strong element of subjectivity from the referee. Referees have to work to make their interpretation of the rules as uniform as possible, yet, in recent years, the introduction of some new rules has increased the interpretative element of the referee's work, consequently the likelihood of subjectivity is higher.

The offside rule is an obvious example here as the referee's interpretation is decisive in determining whether a player is interfering with play or not, whether he will gain an advantage from the situation, or whether he is in any way impeding the opposing goalkeeper. The same goes for judging an 'obvious goal-scoring opportunity'. To decide whether an opportunity is a goal-scoring one, and whether it is obvious or not, the referee has to take into consideration factors that go well beyond the mere knowledge of the rules. He has to refer to a series of experiences that are inevitably subjective, that are difficult to share with others and which certainly do not favour the attainment of that much sought-after uniformity of judgement.

But if it is true that knowledge of the rules of the game is indispensable for the referee, the protagonists of the match ought to know them as well – players, coaches and managers. Very often, however, the questions put to us on the pitch, or the comments made after the match regarding our decisions, make it clear that this is not the case.

Psychological training

Athletic training, together with improving one's knowledge of the rules and the tactical side of the game, does not cover all the preparatory work that a referee can do to perform at his best. At least some consideration has to be given to the time that comes before and after going out onto the pitch – in other words, psychological preparation. Here we really are in a most subjective area, because mental preparation for a match varies from referee to referee, just as it does from player to player. I remember being told stories about the great referee, Luigi Agnolin. He used to arrive at the stadium, lie down on the massage bed and sleep for thirty to forty minutes. When I was at the beginning of my career, Agnolin was my role-model, and so I tried to imitate him to the extent of copying his pre-match habits – was he not, after all, one of the best referees in the world? I stretched out on the massage bed and tried to get to sleep. In truth I didn't really manage to, but in any case the effect of that siesta was that I got up feeling completely out of sorts, my only clear feeling being that this was not the psychological approach that suited me.

There are referees who start their mental preparation for a match from the moment they are appointed, forty-eight hours or even a week before. There are others who start only when they reach the stadium. There are referees who in their search for concentration stop speaking completely from the instant they enter the stadium, others who find it by laughing and joking right up until the last minute.

It's a matter of instinct, of character, of mentality, in the end it's a completely subjective matter.

For me the key moment is the meeting with my assistants and the fourth official immediately after lunch, during which we discuss the match and try to imagine all the possible scenarios, taking into account the teams' and the players' characteristics. This is the moment when my match starts, even though there are still three hours to go before kick-off, and everything I do from then on is geared to the match.

Whatever an individual referee's habits might be, when he goes onto the pitch his mental attention has to be concentrated on that match. His mind has to be there completely, especially because the first moments of a match can be the most critical ones. Indeed, an episode that takes place in the first minute can be very difficult to judge because the normal psychological reaction is that a game should begin gently and progressively increase in intensity, so you can therefore gradually adapt your attention level. But when 'something' happens right after kick-off, you have to be ready to react immediately and if you don't have the mental preparation and a high level of concentration, then this is impossible.

The same thing applies for the players. It's no coincidence that one of the most frequent criticisms that managers make of their players is that they haven't gone onto the pitch with their concentration level at 100 per cent. This can lead to them giving away a goal in the first minutes due to a stupid lack of attention.

It sounds obvious that concentration has to be maintained for the whole match, but, on some occasions, the match is going so smoothly, everything's going so well, that a certain level of relaxation, a lowering of concentration might creep in. You can bet your bottom dollar that it's at that precise moment that something important will happen, catching you unaware and unable to make the right decision.

You have to get used to not being distracted, to not being affected by factors outside of the field of play, and this is something you can train for. To be able to isolate yourself from everything that's around you, from the awareness that you're refereeing a match being watched on television by billions of people, from the pressure exerted by 80,000 spectators on the terraces of a stadium, is imperative to be able to provide a good performance.

Experience is a great help, but equally important is to learn to concentrate purely on what one is doing, isolating oneself from everything else. You can practise this while training by concentrating intensely on the movements or exercises that you are doing, only and exclusively on those, to the point where you hear and feel nothing of what is going on around you.

Concentrating on what you're doing also helps in picking up, in perceiving, the nuances that can then help you understand certain situations better. It's very important to develop this and you can train for it in everyday life, by trying to pay maximum attention to the things that happen around you – to the movement of the people around you, to their relationship with others. The referee has to have a wide-ranging peripheral vision that picks up even the smallest of things.

Psychologically speaking, the recovery phase is equally important. The mental energy that is consumed during a match is remarkable. It's true that over the course of a match you run and exert yourself, but it is also undeniable that you consume great quantities of mental energy because the concentration and the tension involve considerable effort. Physically you can recover by sleeping, perhaps helping things along as many people do, and as I do, with a few drops of a sleeping draught. I really admire those who are able to get to sleep with ease after a match. My own experience is that if I get to bed after an evening game (though, in truth, it doesn't make much of a difference if it's an afternoon match) I have trouble getting to sleep before five in the morning. The adrenaline, mixed with the muscular tiredness, means that I toss and turn all night. For this reason, if I'm in Italy after an evening match, I travel back home in the car without running any risk of falling asleep at the wheel, though if I'm abroad, and I have to leave the next day, I take a few drops to make sure I manage to sleep a bit.

I think the best method of recovery is reached by trying to dedicate a few hours to oneself. Sometimes it can be useful to throw yourself into your work, because perhaps you might find some distraction in the post-match discussions, especially if the match didn't go well. However, you have to be really careful of not piling fatigue onto fatigue, whether it be mental or physical. I have the good fortune to live in a seaside town and a few hours of complete freedom on a Monday morning for a walk along the seafront or on the beach, or to sit reading a book, constitutes the best way I know of unwinding and recharging my batteries.

Speaking the same language

In my wide-ranging idea of what training constitutes, I include everything that a referee can do to make sure he speaks the same language as those who are with him on the pitch.

This doesn't simply mean, as I mentioned before, speaking the language of football – knowing what the players are doing on the field – but it also means, quite literally, using the same words, speaking in a way that they can understand. Knowledge of foreign languages is important because a mutual lack of understanding can cause the worst possible results. Body language certainly helps, but I think that the possibility of exchanging a few words in the same language as the players is much more useful.

FIFA and UEFA's decision to insist that international referees be capable of expressing themselves in the most widely used language – English – is a step in that direction, and if possible that should be supported by knowledge of some other language. It's precisely for this reason that for some years now, during our placements at Coverciano, we've all been required to attend a course of English language lessons.

I speak English, Spanish and a bit of French so it's relatively easy for me to communicate with the players during international matches. Sometimes, in the middle of a match, there are moments when it's important to be able to say something, to explain a decision, perhaps even to make a joke that might relieve the tension. To be able to do this confidently is a great help. Whenever there is a lack of communication I feel a sense of helplessness.

Often this need to communicate isn't seen by those who follow football and they think the real reason why languages are useful is so that the referee can understand the players' insults and their swearwords. Of course it's not like that at all, in fact it would often be better not to understand what a player is saying. Once a foreign player who had excellent Italian started complaining to me in my native tongue; after a while I asked him to switch back to German because at least that way I couldn't understood what he was saying.

Neither a traffic policeman nor an actor

I'm a firm supporter of the idea that one of the most important characteristics of today's referee is his ability to communicate. One of the referees who most impressed me during the World Cup finals in Italy in 1990 was Erik Fredricksson, a Swedish referee. This was not so much for his technical ability as for how he managed to communicate. He used gestures extremely effectively – his decisions were always easily understood. You might not have agreed with it, but there was never any doubt about the decision itself and why he'd made it.

Since it's crucial for someone who's playing in a match to understand what's happening on the pitch, Fredricksson's behaviour seems to me to have corresponded perfectly to this requirement. To know immediately what the referee's decision is, in whose favour and perhaps even why, is a great help for the players. A match is also a show for those who are watching it, and the spectator has the right to understand what has been decided on the pitch. In the United States, where this element is very important, the leader of the American foot ball refereeing team has a microphone that's connected to the stadium's PA system which he uses to explain his decision.

Fredricksson's use of gestures went somewhat against common practice in Italy at that time. At that time if a referee moved his arms to indicate the direction of a foul, someone in the crowd would invariably shout, 'You're not a traffic policeman, you're a referee.'

Since then many things have changed and today a certain type of communication through gestures is now commonly used: referees now resemble Fredricksson of the 1990s much more than the Italian referees of the same period.

Sometimes people ask me if I 'act' when I referee, if I'm really the same person both on and off the pitch. I don't believe that during the intensity of a match, in which all your attention is concentrated on every single moment and the pressure is high, you can possibly have time to think about the pose you ought to strike or how to appear any different to how you normally are. However, very often on the pitch you do things or you strike poses that you're simply unaware of and it's only later when you see yourself on television that you see these things.

There is no difference between the man and the referee, on the pitch everyone is just as he is in life, with the same characteristics, the same good and bad points. The idea that a referee might find some means of making up for being weak or frustrated off the pitch when he is on it, is way off the mark: after all, how could a weak person do all that a referee is expected to do before, during and after a match?

Having said this, during the UEFA training sessions we were shown some film (certainly not as an example to follow) taken from a match I refereed during Euro 2000 – Czech Republic–Holland. To put it mildly, my demeanour with the Czech player Tomas Repka is not exactly cordial. Well, every time I see that video, I wonder if that's really me on the screen.

Evaluation

An analysis of your own performance on the pitch can also play an important part in a referee's training, particularly regarding his preparation. There is no one better placed than the referee himself to make this evaluation, so long as he wants to do so in a serious, constructive way and does not just say 'God, how good was I?' every time he sees a video of one of his matches. Watching yourself and judging yourself on video is a crucial part of evaluation: it means checking whether the work you'd done in preparing for the match was enough, whether your preparation could have been improved or whether it proved to be inadequate.

A few years ago UEFA introduced an evaluation system called self-assessment, which obliged each referee to watch recordings of his matches and then produce a summary based on his evaluation, highlighting points of particular interest. This was a stimulating exercise and, in the same way as the group analysis of matches during the World Cup, was extremely useful. Collective discussion of the events of a match doesn't mean highlighting particular referee's mistakes, but shows others how to avoid making the same mistake in the future. It's all too easy to stop at 'everything went well. I did a good job'. That way you improve very little and you develop slowly. Instead, it is important to be very critical with yourself and try to work out whether what you've done during the match was enough, and in those cases where it wasn't, to try to understand why not, and then correct matters.

To help with this process, slow-motion video is very important for referees. Watching your own match and seeing again and again an incident in detail helps you understand whether you made a mistake and if so, why you made it. This is a deeper kind of analysis than appears on television programmes. While they concentrate on the fact that a mistake was made, a referee, on the other hand, is more interested in discovering why the mistake was made and what he can do to make sure it doesn't happen again. This is the only way of developing.

Any evaluation of performance must be seen in the context of training. An 'unlucky' incident, even if it becomes important because it influenced a result, can certainly happen, but in my self-assessment it ends up being of minor importance. If I make a decision based on what I saw at the time and my own preparation was solid, but later the cameras show something different, then I can't do any more than say 'it's happened', and not worry about it too much. The important thing is that I am in the right position to be able to make the decision, and if this is later proved to be wrong by a camera in a position I could never have reached, then there's very little I can do about it.

The player who trains well during the week, who's in top form and then, by chance, makes a mistake, has to view this mistake in the light of his own preparation. If his preparation was good and the mistake was an unfortunate one, then he has to know how to accept it and not let his game be affected. For players, as for referees, it's not the importance of the mistake itself that defines the whole evaluation. For both categories the right to make mistakes has to be recognized and upheld and it is only a lack of preparation that warrants self-criticism and correction.

Unfortunately for the referee, a good performance, a well-directed match, can be completely wiped out by a decision that might be extremely difficult or even impossible to make or one which only a camera can prove was a mistake. This is the main reason why there is often very little harmony between an 'external' evaluation and a referee's self-evaluation. I tend to concentrate more on aspects of the game that others have simply put to one side or have even ignored as they focus on incidents that I file away in a folder marked 'chance'.

I don't mean to take any importance away from external evaluation, because seeing the same thing with different eyes does increase one's own knowledge. It's precisely for this reason that in Italy today every match played, from Serie C upwards, is observed and evaluated by ex-referees who are sent out to the various stadiums with this sole purpose. They discuss the match with the referee and draw up a report in which the referee's performance is analysed in a detailed, precise manner. These analyses are important because they show the growth of a referee and the development of his career.

Although the observers are important, I remain convinced, however, that there is no one better placed than the referee himself to evaluate his own performance, so long as he can adopt an objective and critical stance with regard to his own game.

Group work

One of the moments when the various phases of training come together is during the 'retreats' to which the Serie A and B referees are periodically called.

In the summer period before the beginning of the championship, we all go on a retreat of some twelve days. There referees and assistants train twice a day and attend a series of technical lessons, some of which are the same for everybody, while others are divided between assistants and referees. We all come to this meeting with some three or four weeks' worth of training under our belts because for us the retreat isn't the beginning of our training as it is for football teams. In this period, usually at the beginning of the month of August, basic work is carried out, principally on speed and speed-related stamina, and at the end of it the Italian Cup starts.

The days are very intense and normally involve getting up between 07.30 and 8.00 and having breakfast, then at 09.30 beginning the morning session which ends at 11.00. We shower and then at 12.00 there is a technical lesson followed by lunch at 13.00 and rest until 16.00. There is a second technical meeting from 16.30 to 17.30 and a second train ing session between 18.00 and 19.30. At 20.30 supper and then to bed because by that stage you're truly shattered.

Right from the day before the championship starts and then throughout the season, we are called to take part in a series of training sessions, normally every fortnight, but depending on the schedule, sometimes for several weeks in a row. We therefore look on the top-level facilities of the Federation's technical centre at Coverciano as a second home.

Arrival there is generally scheduled for the Thursday evening and the first thing that happens on the Friday morning is the weigh-in, a ritual now in every sense. Friday and Saturday mornings are dedicated to a training session, with different loads and intensities according to whether or not each referee might have a match that weekend. Over the course of the season we have to undergo tests on our physical fitness.

Much of the remaining time is then dedicated to technical work, during which, with the help of videotapes, the most significant situations of the two previous days are analysed and the referee panel provides the interpretation that should then become common to the entire group.

The trainer's work is particularly important during these meetings. With him we discuss tactics and technique, both generally and with specific reference to the individual games that we'll be refereeing. The referees who don't have matches at the weekend then take part in a special training session on the Friday afternoon, a session that consists of a game of football – played to the death.

These methods, both extremely interesting and at the cutting edge in terms of referee training, are producing excellent results, to the extent that other associations in other countries, after seeing what we do, have decided to adopt similar approaches.

But above and beyond the purely technical benefits, we're enjoying excellent results in attaining a greater group and team mentality.

The referee has always been an individual who plays his match by himself, at the most relying on the other members of his team. But by spending so much time together we're acquiring a sort of team spirit, a group approach and that's a great help not only for us, but for football as a whole.

Three

Build-Ups and Preliminaries

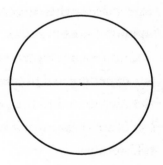

Postcards and phone calls

The moment that has always excited me most, as it does most referees, is the moment when the match I'll be refereeing is assigned to me – the now famous 'appointment'.

The appointment has always been made, as in almost all countries in the world, by a committee mostly made up of ex-referees who choose the most suitable referee in their opinion for each match. This decision takes many factors into account – the degree of difficulty associated with the match, the experience of the referee and his state of fitness – basically the idea is to find the perfect referee for each match.

In some countries, however, the appointment is now made differently.

In Spain, for example, a computer decides at the beginning of the season who will referee which matches for the entire championship. To make everything fair, the rules stipulate that referees cannot direct matches involving teams from his region, that there should be some turnover and that each referee has the same number of matches. The appointments remain secret and are published week by week.

A similar system has recently been introduced in Italy.

Initially it covered the entire championship with referees being given a combination of randomly selected Serie A and Serie B matches. Now it is organized in 'bands' into which the Serie A and Serie B matches are divided, for which there are two corresponding bands of referees. In this way, chance has taken the place of an appointment based on a considered opinion regarding each individual referee's abilities and his suitability for each match.

Given my role, for me to express preferences or judgements would not be the right thing to do, but I don't think I'm wrong to say that no one facing an operation would ever leave their choice of surgeon to chance, neither would a manager draw lots for his team's match line-up. A rational choice should always prevail over a matter of luck.

It might seem strange, but waiting to know where I'll be going to referee on Sunday is almost more exciting than the match itself, and once I know which match I've been appointed to, it's almost as though I've already refereed it.

For me the 'pleasure' of the appointment doesn't derive from the league in which I referee or the importance of the match. It's the same pleasure that's accompanied me ever since I started refereeing my first matches. I wasn't even eighteen and I waited for the day when the postman delivered the letter (appointments were sent out by post back then) telling me which match I was to referee like a child waiting for Father Christmas. On coming back home from school the first thing I asked my parents was whether the postman had brought anything – if he'd delivered the express letter. And ever since then the ritual has been repeated, although the means used now are different. When I was in the amateur leagues the envelope with the appointment also contained the report that had to be drawn up at the end of the game. The sheets of the report were different colours for each league and, like a poker player slowly fanning out his cards, I would open the envelope in my own good time so that I could see from the colour of the report – pink, light blue, or yellow – whether I was to be refereeing in the Promotion, First or Second division.

Then, as I moved up the ladder, the envelope was replaced by a phone call to the appointments committee in Rome. You called them and they let you know which match was yours. This method was used right up to the highest level and was still in place until just a few years ago. A phone call full of trepidation and suspense, which often led to some considerable satisfaction – for example an appointment to a top match – or moments of great disappointment whenever the committee's administrative staff said that you were free that Sunday – it was the same sort of feeling as when the postman had nothing for you.

When we're at Coverciano, we receive the appointments directly after the Friday morning training session. During the session, however, the first news of the draw leaks out and finds its way onto the training ground.

Personally, if I could, I'd be out there on the pitch every Sunday and I'm sure the same thing is true for all referees –

in fact, I'd bet on it. The same thing goes for players: no one likes sitting in the stands or on the bench. Even though sometimes you inevitably feel tired and rationally you say to yourself that a rest, some relaxation, might be useful, neither footballers nor referees like sitting back and watching. This was especially true back in the days of what we used to call (using the English word) 'turnover', when every other week you were rested. The frustration of waiting for the next match used to get to me and I was always happier when I happened to have two or three matches in a row. I was convinced back then, and I remain so now, that the more consecutive games a referee has, then the better chance he has of being in good physical shape. At the end of the day, all the work we do is geared towards the match so it's obvious that all we want to do is get out on the pitch.

Receiving your appointment was always followed, particularly when I was refereeing in the youth or the amateur leagues, by another intense phase of preparation – planning the trip. This meant serious consultation of road maps or train time tables, studying information on hotels and restaurants and searching for the best way to reach such and such a place. The referee had to use his own initiative to make these arrangements and, while today these things are more or less taken care of, back then it was a voyage of discovery, a way of seeing new places and different cities.

I've travelled to towns that otherwise I'd never have seen and thanks to this I've become quite an expert in Italian geography. I remember quite clearly how my friends would make fun of me as I set off for some out-of-the-way destination knowing full well that, instead of being with them, I'd be spending Saturday night on my own, perhaps at the cinema or in front of the television in a hotel room.

Today it's all much easier and most of the places I go to I've visited many times, so the hotels and restaurants are generally familiar.

For international matches things are slightly different and I still get to travel to new places and, even though the journeys are organized for us by UEFA or FIFA, we do get the chance to tailor things to our own requirements. Thanks to the Internet, I can now play at being my own travel agent.

Sometimes it really takes imagination to stop a journey becoming a logistical nightmare. In September 1996, immediately following the Atlanta Olympics, I was appointed to a World Cup qualifying match to be played between Armenia and Germany in Erevan, Armenia's capital. The match was on a Wednesday and the FIFA travel agent suggested that I should leave on the Sunday from Milan, fly to Moscow and from there travel on to Erevan, taking a return flight to Italy on the Friday. Five nights away from home in Armenia seemed a bit much to me and so, after hours of research, I managed to find an outbound flight on the Monday via Sofia with an overnight stopover. The journey back would start just three hours after the match – a flight from Erevan to Paris, in the middle of the night, followed by a connection to Pisa. Despite the plane that took us from Sofia to Erevan looking like it might fall apart any minute, this solution proved to be much better, not least because of the quality of the hotel I was booked into.

When I tell people about my life as a referee, especially regarding the international matches, they always think that my trips are an opportunity to visit cities and to 'see the world'. Unfortunately, things aren't like that. I've become an expert on airports, on hotels and stadiums, but I've learned very little about the cities. It's not just due to a lack of time, but it's also because the idea of being a referee 'tourist' doesn't exactly fit in with my way of seeing things.

When we're abroad for a match, as soon as we arrive in an airport we're picked up by a minder from the home association, often an ex-referee, who'll then take care of us throughout our stay. The first thing is to get to the hotel. In the late afternoon I try to get some training in, if possible in the stadium where the match will be played, which means that my training has to suit the scheduled times for the teams' training. I find this useful for shaking off the fatigue accumulated during the journey, particularly if it's been a long one, and to start getting a feel for the place where the match will be played. After that it's supper and then to bed. At around 9.30 on the morning of match day, there's an inspection at the ground and a safety briefing that the referee takes part in, together with assistants, the fourth official, the teams' representatives and all those who are involved in the match: police, fire brigade, doctors and first-aiders. During this meeting all the details regarding the organization of the match are discussed, particularly in terms of safety. The referee then checks the colours of the strips the two teams will be wearing.

We're left to our own devices by about 11.00 and lunch is usually at 12.30, so there's generally little more than an hour to get to see a couple, literally a couple, of things in the city. The afternoon is dedicated to rest, then there's the match and then the following morning there's the journey back home to Italy.

As you can see, there's not much scope for sightseeing. But sometimes, especially when I'm in a place that I probably won't be travelling to again in the near future, I manage to organize a little excursion. In Moscow, for example, I managed to see Red Square and the Kremlin; in Uruguay I saw the Rio de la Plata flowing into the Atlantic; in Istanbul I was much taken with the delights of the Topkapi Palace. I once refereed a friendly between China and England and on that occasion I was luckier than usual. I was there for a total of five days and managed to spend at least two and a half days seeing the sights: the Great Wall, the Temple of Heaven, the Forbidden City. It was well worth it – it was an unforgettable experience – but in no way did it distract from my status as a leading expert on airports and hotels.

Those 'special' build-ups

As I have said, all matches are the same, but some are more important than others and each referee has build-ups that he particularly remembers, either because of the importance of the match, or because of something that happened. For me it's the same thing, and of all the build-ups to matches I've had in my career, some remain more clearly impressed on my memory than others. For example, the week following my first appointment to a Serie A match.

By that time I'd already refereed a fair amount of important Serie B matches and I was beginning to hope that I might be appointed to a match in the top division. So it really was a wonderful moment when the then head of the national referees' committee, Paolo Casarin, told me that the following Sunday, 15 December 1991, I'd be off to Verona for Verona– Ascoli: a dream come true.

I was thirty-one years old, and by the standards of the day I was decidedly young for Serie A, the ultimate ambition that an Italian referee can realistically have in his career. If you then have the chance to go further then that is an extra ordinary achievement, but such things cannot be planned rationally. Whatever, one of the clearest memories I have of my build-up to Serie A, apart from my excitement, con cerns the organization of that journey. Thanks to a kind of 'mentoring' programme, I'd been assigned two of the most famous and expert assistants of that time – Ramicone and Andreozzi – both from the Lazio region and both used to the limelight. Obviously I'd never worked with either of them before. I thought the most convenient way of getting to Verona from Rome was on the plane and so, since I had to organize the journey for them as well, I asked them if they wanted me to pick them up at the airport. They promptly rejected my idea in favour of the train without giving a particular reason why. It was only after a series of attempts at persuading them that I learnt that one of them, Ramicone, was terrified of the very idea of getting on a plane and so used the train even for the longest journeys. After all, if Dennis Bergkamp has a clause in his contract with Arsenal stipulating that he can miss away games that involve flying, then Ramicone was perfectly at liberty to go to Rome on the train . . . all he had to do was let me know.

The match finished 1–0 to Verona and the reports were all positive. After the match as we were walking out of Verona's Bentegodi stadium, Casarin gave an interview. He was very flattering and the expression on my face as I stood next to him was like a kid who'd just eaten his favourite ice-cream.

Other special build-ups include those before big finals, such as the Atlanta Olympics in 1996. That was a real surprise because I was one of the youngest referees in the Olympic tournament and had been working at the international level for only a year. I knew I'd performed well, that I'd refereed some good matches, but in all sincerity I really didn't think I was among those who could realistically hope to referee the final. Gradually, as we got nearer to the end of the tournament, the number of referees diminished and as I continued to be excluded from those appointed to the quarter-and semi-finals, I began to think that perhaps I was one of the possible candidates.

In situations like this you never know whether to be happy or not. Every time the appointments for a phase of a tournament are made public, and your name isn't on the list, you feel a combination of disappointment and satisfaction. On the one hand you're unhappy because nobody likes standing around and watching and you're not sure you're going to be refereeing in one of the later stages, but on the other, there's the hope that you might get one of the closing games, perhaps even the final.

Things were slightly different at the last World Cup. I had greater expectations and so the element of surprise was no longer there: in 2002 I was among the most experienced referees and was part of that small group that could hope to officiate in the final.

Given that my performances had been well received, Italy had been knocked out at the group stage and I wasn't used in the quarter-finals, I knew that I had a chance to referee the final. At that point, everyone around you seems to know everything and you receive a series of phone calls from the usual well-connected types who tell you, 'Listen, it's all sorted out, the final is yours, believe me, no doubt whatsoever.' However, being very practical, I always have doubts in these cases. I like to be certain before celebrating an appointment to a match and so always wait to receive the official confirmation. I stuck to this in Japan and over the days before the appointment became official, which was on the morning of Thursday 27 June, I took nothing for granted, not even when speaking with my wife, my friends and the members of the referees' panel back in Italy. In fact I tried to dampen the enthusiasm of those who really were taking it for granted. Perhaps this attitude also comes from a mild dose of superstition, which never goes amiss in such cases.

During that time, rumours were coming from Italy about my unsuitability for the final because of the fuss over my participation in an Adidas publicity campaign – of the two finalists Germany were sponsored by Adidas and Brazil by Nike. It's incredible that this sort of thing could be considered about a referee, but not about the players. And don't say anything about referees having to project some special image of being above suspicion, because I should be judged for *what* I do and not for what people *think* I do.

The committee meeting that had to choose the referees for the two finals began at eight in the morning in the Tokyo hotel where FIFA headquarters was set up. After the meeting was over, some of the committee members came back to the hotel where we were based and I thought someone might say, 'Can we have your attention for a minute – we're going to tell you who's been chosen.' It would have made sense, if for no other reason than to relieve a bit of the tension that had inevitably built up. We all kept trying to look indifferent, but every one of us was poised, trying to pick up any hint or signal in the faces of those 'in the know'. But there was nothing doing, the only communication was that the official announcement would come at 14.30 hours, another hour of waiting.

The fateful hour finally arrived and we were called into the room where the match analysis usually took place. For some unknown reason there were no chairs in there at that moment and so we all sat on the floor, our backs against the wall. Chance had it that the other referee who, in my opinion, had all the credentials for refereeing the final, Anders Frisk, from Sweden, was sitting right next to me and he was the first to congratulate me when I was told that I had been appointed. Although he had every right to think he might have refereed the match, I think he'd probably persuaded himself that he wasn't going to get it.

After my colleagues' congratulations, and a hug for the other members of the team for the final, the external 'celebrations' began: phone calls home, official confirmation and then the real 'torture'. Over the following six hours the whole world seemed to phone me, everyone asking for something – a comment, an opinion, a statement. For a whole day the press officer worked almost exclusively for me and I have to say that speaking for hours on the phone with journalists from all over the world was really tiring. Luckily FIFA put a deadline on 'external' contact – midday on the Friday, immediately after the official press conference at the Yokohama Media Centre. That was it. From then on everyone's mind had to be on the match and the match alone.

You can't always win

But build-ups don't always lead to refereeing a final. Sometimes your expectations, your hopes, are shattered. That's happened to me before – for example in the World Cup in France in 1998 when, under the rules then in force, the referees whose national teams had qualified for the quarter-finals were automatically 'let go', a euphemism for their elimination from the competition.

Italy played their first match after the group stage against Norway. I watched it with the Norwegian referee Rune Pedersen and at the end he congratulated me warmly on Italy's victory, probably without realizing that at that moment he was saying goodbye because the victory meant my exit from the tournament. Rune is an extraordinary person, but those congratulations coincided with my disappointment at the certain end of my tournament. The next day France eliminated Paraguay; the referee in the room next to mine was from the host nation – another friend and great character, Marc Batta of Marseilles. At the end of that match I knocked on his door and said, 'So, what shall we do? Pack our bags?' And he replied, 'I think so . . . I really think we can start getting our stuff ready.'

The home referee's information was true, so I began planning not my return to Italy, but a three or four day holiday with my wife in Paris. I'd experienced the tournament as a referee and now I was going to be a spectator, so we went together to see France–Italy, the quarter-final at the Stade de France in Saint Denis. Apart from the spectacle itself – the crowd and the atmosphere were magnificent – the final result, with Italy being defeated on penalties, simply added my disappointment as a supporter to my disappointment as a referee.

This also happened in Euro 2000 in Belgium and Holland. I had been appointed to the France–Spain quarter-final and the evening before the match Italy played their quarter-final with Romania. I watched the game in the Bruges hotel where I was based and when Italy won I knew for certain that the next day's match was to be my last of the tournament. The official confirmation, however, wouldn't come until the end of all the quarter-finals when we were all back at headquarters in Brussels and the committee had officially decided. These were the rules and I sought to do my best, perhaps even more than usual, because it was my last chance in the tournament to show what I could do.

Even though you're prepared for it, you still think there might be a glimmer of hope. 'Who knows?' you irrationally think to yourself, 'Perhaps they've changed the rules . . .' But it doesn't work like that, and it hurts a bit when you read the list of referees who are to stay and your name isn't on it. That moment when you leave the meeting to get your bags ready and say goodbye to everyone you've worked with over the tournament is both sad and difficult.

But this all fades away when you realize that this means

you're going to see your family again. It's the same feeling I had during the last World Cup, except in reverse, as the joy of staying on was spoiled somewhat by knowing that I would have to be away from home for longer. Just before the tournament Christian Panucci, the Italian player, gave an interview and a journalist asked him, 'What do you think this experience will be like?' And he replied 'It'll be a great experience . . . wonderful. At the professional level, playing in the World Cup is the ultimate, but a long time away from home will get everyone down.' I agree with every word. The forty-two days spent in Japan, while splendid in terms of hospitality and professional satisfaction, were heavy-going because of the distance from home.

My build-up for the Champions' League final in 1999, on the other hand, was a bit more complicated and a little solitary.

Since 1991, there had always been an Italian club in the Champions' League final, so Italian referees were always automatically excluded. In the 1998–99 season Juventus reached the semi-final, and it looked again as though there was no hope for me as a referee. Juventus drew 1–1 in the first leg at Manchester and consequently had the second leg at home. Everything looked set for their qualification for the final in Barcelona. After just a few minutes of the match in Turin, Juventus scored and when they scored again it looked as though the game was over. But Manchester United came back and won 3–2, thus qualifying for the final with Bayern Munich – a game that could finally go to an Italian referee. At that time

I was the Italian referee with the best track record, having just completed a very positive season at the European level. But what I thought was going to be a very straightforward decision was turned into something far more complicated by the then president of the Italian referees' association, and member of UEFA's referees' panel, Sergio Gonella. He told me explicitly that, in his opinion, I stood no chance. I was very put out and couldn't work out why he was being so negative. To this day I still have no idea what happened, but the fact is that in the space of a couple of weeks my disappointment was transformed into one of the greatest and most satisfying moments of my career. I was appointed to the final of the Champions' League, a match that's the equivalent of the World Cup at club level. Two of the most prestigious teams in Europe in one of the best stadiums, the Nou Camp in Barcelona, in my favourite European city. It had been a difficult build-up, but the outcome was certainly worth it.

Always away

But let's get back to build-ups in the strictest sense of the word – to the days and hours before a match. So many Saturday nights spent in restaurants on my own! And I hate eating alone, it really gets me down. I can honestly say that going into a restaurant, sitting down and eating alone is, for me, a vision of hell. It's comparable only to going to the cinema on your own, especially on a Saturday evening, when 'normal' people usually go out in company. And I've spent many an evening at the cinema on my own.

It was quite common to be appointed to matches that were some distance from home and so you had to set off on the Saturday, while the assistants usually came from the local area and would turn up on the Sunday morning. The only alternatives then were eating in your room in front of the television or reading a book. Today the situation is much improved in that the assistants always arrive the night before and you don't have to spend the Saturday evening on your own.

But solitude is not just a matter of circumstance. During the build-up you need peace and quiet, after I have got to know my team-mates, the assistants, then I need to get into my pre-match rhythm, with all my habits and little rituals. The same habits, the same things, the same actions, often the same thoughts, which explains why I often choose quiet hotels. And I've often chosen – especially when my children were very young – to sleep in a hotel even when the matches are played in towns near where I live – for example Lucca, whose stadium is no more than twenty minutes in the car from my home. My wife has never come with me to a match because her presence would upset my routine.

Despite my being so careful about which hotel I choose, there was one occasion when things went a bit wrong. It was my debut in Serie C1, in Venice for the match Venezia Mestre–Carrarese. I'd booked my own hotel and arrived there on a very foggy Saturday night. I walked into the lobby and the first person I met was the manager of the Tuscan team. I was a bit taken aback and thought to myself, 'What's he doing here?' He explained to me that the fog had meant that the team hadn't been able to get to the hotel they'd booked and mine had proved to be the nearest one. I felt that changing hotels at that stage would have caused more problems than actually staying. I informed the Referees' Committee and so we spent the remaining time before the match avoiding one another. During the evening there was no problem, but the following day, at lunchtime, they set up tables in two different areas with a sort of screen between us. Thus we managed to respect the rules as well as my reluctance, irrespective of whether I have to referee or not, to spend lots of time sitting down to eat.

Two 'different' build-ups

Sometimes the build-up can become problematic. This happened to me a couple of years ago, right in the midst of another, more important, build-up – the build-up to Christmas. The match was on 23 December – Napoli–Parma at the San Paolo stadium. I'd decided to stay at home for as long as possible and then take the last plane from Pisa with a stop in Rome before arriving in the evening in Naples. There was an assistant with me from Lucca, Marcello Gini, while the other assistant was due to come up to Naples from the south. As always when I take the last flight in the evening, my plan was to eat between flights in Rome's Fiumicino airport, but the assistant, who was someone I trained with and was also getting ready to retire, said to me, 'Come on, for once let's not eat in the airport, let's go and eat in Naples.' I didn't want to disappoint him, he's a friend, and so I accepted: 'All right then, as soon as we get there we'll go straight to Ciro's at Mergellina, without even stopping off at the hotel. As long as we're quick.' We landed on time and took a taxi to Ciro's. We still had our coats on as we ordered, specifying that they had to bring the food as quickly as possible, and then I went to the bathroom to wash my hands. I was in such a rush that I didn't notice the doorframe – it was much lower than they usually are – and after a tremendous thump I found myself on the floor. The first thing I felt was something hot and wet on the top of my head; I put my hand up to the hot spot and brought it down covered in blood. I sat there listening to the drip, drip of the drops on the floor. I then called for help and someone arrived with some ice. There then ensued an animated discussion among all the onlookers, one to which I had no significant contribution to make. I was concentrating on my own pain when I heard my assistant's voice, 'The ice will sort it all out.' My head was really hurting and some of the onlookers were suggesting it was nothing, others were recommending a trip to the hospital for some stitches.

The discussion continued until someone remembered that there was a plastic surgeon eating in the restaurant that evening. The doctor interrupted his meal, came to take a look and announced, 'The wound is quite big, you'd best have it stitched.' Had I gone to hospital for stitches the night before the match, then the next day it would have been all over the papers, creating all sorts of fuss, and so I asked if there wasn't perhaps some other solution. Fortunately the owner of the restaurant managed to convince the surgeon to go to his car, which was parked some twenty minutes or so away, fetch his bag and come back to 'operate' on me in a private room in the restaurant, under a lamp. Six stitches, a neat job with no scar, and, thanks to a couple of skin-coloured elastoplasts, no one noticed anything the next day, not even with the closest of television close-ups.

The moral of this tale is that now, when I decide to eat in Fiumicino, I eat in Fiumicino, without being swayed by anyone's wishes.

Another 'different' sort of build-up didn't really involve a match as much as it involved the birth of my second daughter, Carolina. I don't know if my wife had deliberately miscalculated dates and so forth, but the birth was due to take place at the beginning of April. So as not to run any risk of missing the event, I'd decided not to referee the final phase of an international under-18 tournament in Belgium. After that I pulled out of a couple of league games, but there was still no sign of Carolina. Then, some weeks after the supposed date of birth, I asked to be given an appointment and promptly received Cagliari–Padova. Obviously, before committing myself to travelling to Sardinia, with another referee already on standby, my wife and I went to see the obstetrician. After studying the monitor printout he declared emphatically, 'Nothing's going to happen before Wednesday or Thursday. Your wife can go back home and you can travel without worrying about anything.' I took my wife back home, went to the airport and set off for Cagliari, happy with what the doctor had said. I called home from the hotel – everything was all right and I slept peacefully. At seven thirty in the morning my mother-in-law phoned to congratulate me on becoming a father for the second time around.

I'm not the only referee to have experienced this, which is something that testifies to the commitment we have to what we do, even to the point of missing moments as important as this one.

At the stadium

Let's now consider the hours and events immediately before the match. Obviously the referee's build-up, just like the player's build-up, is not the same as the supporter's. The referee's build-up consists of concentration, and although I'm quite good at 'switching off' and keeping calm and relaxed, from lunch onwards my aim is simply to reach the highest possible levels of concentration. The jokes come to an end and it's time to think of nothing but the match. If there isn't enough peace and quiet, I look for it. I can't bear it when someone starts kicking a ball against the walls of the dressing room. I avoid confusion and disorder in all their forms, even those that might come from a 'mistake' in laying out my kit or the various objects I need on the pitch.

Referees, myself included, normally get to the stadium about an hour and a half before the match, although I might on occasions turn up fifteen minutes earlier even than that. For the World Cup final, the assistants and I arrived two and a half hours beforehand, very early indeed, because the Emperor of Japan was due to arrive some two hours before kick-off and from that point onwards everything around the stadium was going to be blocked. We had to be there before him, and this meant we had much more dressing-room time than usual. But under normal circumstances some ninety minutes before match time are absolutely necessary, even though, don't ask me how, I always end up doing all my final preparations in a real rush.

Although you try to make sure everything is organized, there are times when some unforeseen event can ruin your plans. Once when I was refereeing in Serie C, I very nearly didn't make it to the stadium. I'd been called to referee an important match – Spezia–Lucchese. At that time I was living in Bologna so I was eligible to referee Lucchese, something which today, because I live in Viareggio, I wouldn't be able to do. It really was an important match because at the end of the previous season Lucchese had beaten Spezia on the last day of the championship, denying them promotion to Serie B. Spezia were out for revenge. It just so happened that I'd had my car stolen and so I asked my cousin to lend me his brand-new, red Renault 4. My wife's family lived in Viareggio and so together we set off from Bologna on the Saturday afternoon. I went off in the evening to sleep, professional as I am, in a hotel, while my wife went to stay at her mother's. The next morning I had something to eat and set off in the car. I remember thinking as I was driving towards La Spezia that it really was true what they say about the Renault 4's economic fuel consumption. The gauge was at almost the same level it was at when we'd set off from Bologna. At about twenty kilometres from La Spezia, near Carrara, the engine started spluttering and I just managed to pull over onto the hard shoulder before it conked out completely. I tried to get it going a couple of times and then started hitchhiking – back in those days mobile phones weren't common at all – and I managed to get a lift to the Carrara exit. I found a recovery crew there and when we got back to the car they explained that the tank was completely empty. My little cousin later explained that the gauge was broken. The driver of the recovery truck put some petrol in the tank, I set off again and got to the stadium with just thirty-five minutes to spare before kick-off. The faces of the staff were slightly strained with the worry that the match might have been called off, but despite my late arrival, the game got under way as planned.

For many people getting to the stadium so early seems a bit too much and often the taxi-driver who takes me to the stadium will ask, 'But you're going there already, the match doesn't start until . . .' Maybe it's because people don't think that getting ready for a match takes time. With this in mind, it might be interesting to recount something of what happens in the dressing room.

While every referee has his own habits, in general there are no great differences between them all. The first thing that has to be done when you get to the stadium is to carry out an inspection of the ground – checking the lines, making sure the goals are securely fixed to the ground and that there are no large holes in the nets. For matches played in Italy I generally leave this job to the assistants, while I stay in the dressing room and start getting the 'tools of the trade' ready – my boots, kit, whistle and so on.

Stadium dressing rooms vary a lot: from the enormous and extremely practical, to the tiny and almost impossible for four people to use at the same time. When I first went to Wembley, the world's most famous stadium, I was disappointed to find that our dressing room was really small and poorly furnished, but it was some consolation to see that the players' dressing rooms weren't much better. (Let's hope the new Wembley, being built over the next few years, will be a bit more comfortable.) In Zurich I was surprised to find a small curtain in our dressing room, behind which were a stash of brooms. The dressing rooms in the Santiago Bernabeu Stadium in Madrid, on the other hand, were truly splendid, particularly those of the Real Madrid players, which was a great expanse of space with personalized lockers decorated with almost life-size Plexiglas reproductions of the players themselves.

Usually the arrival at the stadium is a peaceful time, but sometimes unusual or unpleasant things happen in the hours before a match. I once witnessed a pitch invasion more than an hour before kick-off. We were out on the pitch and the home supporters jumped over a fence, not, I might add, with a view to complimenting the visiting team's players. Not exactly the best way to get a match started.

Unfortunately the build-up to matches, particularly in the lower leagues, is a moment that some fans see as an opportunity to intimidate the visiting teams or the referee. I have seen the visitors' coach pelted with missiles that have shattered the windows, the players insulted, the referee threatened, in the vain hope that it might help win the match. It's an unpleasant side of football, difficult to understand, but we can't pretend that it doesn't exist. Indeed, this is further demonstration of the passion that drives a referee. Sometimes you find yourself, especially at the amateur level, in situations where your physical safety is at risk, because anything might happen, regardless of whether or not you referee well. It's only the final result that counts. And recent history records episodes of attacks on referees even in the youth leagues, sometimes perpetrated by players' parents, and if you read the reports of the Sporting Arbiter that describe these events, you really do wonder how it can possibly happen.

If you were to sit down and think rationally about the reasons that lead to you finding yourself in situations like that, well. . . you wouldn't really come up with many answers. And yet, I was always the first to dive in there whenever I was refereeing 'difficult' matches – those in which there was greater risk, where the rivalry between teams, between towns, between neighbourhoods, was highest. I was always 'up for it', because it was something that gave me satisfaction. All referees want to 'take on' the most heated matches – a derby or a match with relegation or promotion at stake, perhaps on some small sun-baked pitch in the south – despite the fact that he knows he's running greater risks. The sense of gratification I felt when they sent me to referee 'the match' of the week, it was like a prize, a recognition, and I paid no heed to the risk involved.

And today when I think back on some of the situations I've been in, the only thing I can say is, 'Mamma mia!' No more, no less, just, 'Mamma mia!'

In the dressing room

But let's imagine that reaching the dressing room has been, as it usually is, straightforward and peaceful. I'm often asked if I have special rituals or superstitions. In truth I'm a methodical person, and if I repeat the same actions every time it's not because they bring me good luck, but rather it's because they're part of my own habits and I think repeating them helps me.

Still, I'm beginning to realize that over time the attention I pay to the repetition of some things becomes, shall we say, less obsessive. Back in 1995 I went as reserve referee for Pierluigi Pairetto in a Bulgaria–Germany Euro qualifier game. He was then the number one Italian referee with lots of experience and I was amazed when I saw him rooting through his bag looking for some personal item he couldn't find. I remember thinking, 'Well, just look at that. That could never happen to me, I'm too disciplined.' But a few years have gone by since then and more than once over this period I've arrived at the stadium to discover that something was missing. Once it was the assistants' flags, and it wasn't in just any game – it was no less than the Champions' League final in Barcelona. Usually in international matches the flags are given to the two assistants right from the start of the away trip, whereas in Italy it's the referee who brings them to the stadium. On that occasion, I don't know why, I kept hold of them and took them to my room in the hotel. Naturally, the following day, I forgot them and it was only when we were in the dressing rooms at the Nou Camp that I realized. There was a moment of sheer panic and then we asked for help from the police – it took just half an hour for the motorcyclist to arrive with the flags.

Whistle, watch, cards, notebook and all the other tools of the trade don't carry particularly superstitious meanings. What I always follow is simply my sense of routine.

Perhaps the only object I actually try to make sure is always with me is a silver half dollar for tossing the coin at the centre circle. There's no really superstitious attachment to this coin, but if I've got it with me I feel better. I remember that after the toss-up for one match – Cesena–Verona in Serie B — I gave it to the fourth official to look after, an assistant from Florence. When we got back to the dressing room I asked him for it and he started feeling in all his pockets and then announced, 'I can't find it.'

'What do you mean you can't find it?'

'Well . . . I've lost it.'

At that point I got everyone out there looking for the half dollar like bloodhounds. No joy though. I have to admit I wasn't at all happy. But then, a week later, I got it back from the Cesena physiotherapist who had been given it by a carabiniere who'd been on duty that day. In the end I think there's more sentiment than superstition in my attachment to my half-dollar.

Usually at about forty-five minutes from kick-off some of the administrators from the teams bring the team sheets and the strips to have the colours checked. The shirts, shorts and socks all have to be of different colours compared to those of the opponents. And, obviously, different from those of the referee.

No more black jackets

Indeed, for some years now referees have been able to choose the colour of the kit they wear, after decades of having been required to wear the classic black jacket. 'Jacket' because it really was in every respect a jacket, with buttons and a white shirt. All that was missing was a tie, but perhaps at the very beginning they wore that as well. This in itself is enough to show just how undervalued the athletic side of the referee's job was. His role as judge was paramount, he may be a judge in shorts, but he needed to be formal and elegant out of respect for his role. Then, gradually, in the 1960s, there was the shift to blouson jackets with long zips, and then today's coloured kit. The day we started refereeing wearing coloured shirts an article of mine was published on the first page of the *Nazione*, Florence's daily newspaper. Being able to choose the colour was to my mind an important sign of freedom, a small but significant concession to the aesthetic independence of each individual referee.

But as is often the case in human nature, we end up coming back to what we know, and today I look upon the black kit as being the most attractive of all, and chose to referee the World Cup final wearing it. Not only is it the most attractive, but it's the smartest as well, lending the referee's image both sobriety and style.

There has also been considerable development in the material used for the kit: the fabrics are state of the art, as are the boots. All this shows that the referee today enjoys new levels of attention and is considered as being another athlete on the pitch.

As I mentioned, the arrival of our coloured kit means that we need to be even more careful about the compatibility of the colours used for the two teams' strips. The ideal situation, although it's not always possible, is that there be no man on the pitch (from the two teams and the refereeing team) who has any element of his kit that's the same colour as any of the others. Up until a few years ago, for example, you might see two opposing teams both wearing black shorts or white socks. That no longer happens today because the increased speed of the game means that players have to be able to distinguish team-mates from opponents, say, from the colour of their socks. And if the referee and assistants have shorts or socks of the same colour then this represents a further difficulty.

Warming up

Almost all of us now use physiotherapists for the initial warming up phase, which is then followed by the real warm-up. Up until a few years ago almost all referees did all of this in the dressing room, managing as best we could. Things have changed now, though, and the routine in Italy is the same as what has always been common practice for international matches – almost all referees warm up on the pitch, just as the players do. Unfortunately people continue to consider the referee in a special sort of light and you still get comments, such as the one I heard not so long ago while I was doing some stretching exercises on the pitch – it wasn't becoming for a referee to be seen in that position.

Each of us warms up using special exercises that differ from referee to referee. For example I start with some light running for five to six minutes with some 'crossing' – lateral or diagonal movements – to which I then add some stretching for muscles and tendons. At this point I move on to speed work with skipping, kicking and sprinting. A bit more stretching and I'm ready. In total it all lasts some twenty minutes.

Ten minutes before kick-off everyone returns to the dressing room, while the fourth official goes to do the roll call of the players. It might seem strange, but even in Serie A, just as in the lower divisions, there's the register to be filled in. Obviously it's not identification of the individual player that's important, but the process is just to check that the players on the list correspond to those who go out onto the pitch and that they each put on the right shirt. Another thing that's checked is the players' kit – no rings, chains, bracelets or anything else that might constitute a danger to themselves or to their opponents. Even though it isn't strictly correct, many referees try to turn a blind eye to certain things, such as those players who don't want to be separated from an earring that's particularly important to them.

In the meantime we see to the last-minute details, including fitting the receiver for the electronic flags. For some years now referee and assistants have been in contact thanks to an electronic signal – a beep or a vibration, which each assistant's flag transmits to the referee. Thanks to this system, when necessary, the assistant can call the referee immediately to point out offsides, fouls or any other infringements.

Out onto the pitch

Out of the dressing room and onto the pitch. At this point too, every stadium has its own features: at the San Siro, for example, you have to go down a long flight of stairs, just like Bologna, where a lift to get down to pitch level wouldn't go amiss. In Naples there's a corridor that's at least 150 metres long, while in Genoa, just one step from the referee's dressing room and you're on the flight of stairs that leads to the pitch.

The walk to the pitch is a moment when you meet people – players, managers, staff. Greetings, handshakes, and a few comments are exchanged. Sometimes you see much hugging between former team-mates who are particularly pleased to see each other again. Then you see the same two out on the pitch going hell for leather as they fight for the ball.

One of the funniest things in the ritual immediately before the whistle is the shaking of hands between the two team captains: even though they've said hello to each other and might have chatted, perhaps even joked, in the minutes before going onto the pitch. But if the function of this is to provide a public reinforcement of respect for each other's roles and recognition of mutual sporting values – the classic 'may the best team win' spirit – then long may it continue.

And while we're considering the shaking of hands, I have

to say that I'd like to see, as happens in other sports such as volleyball and rugby, the two teams lining up at the end of the match to shake hands. That would be the best way to mark the end of the match in true sporting style.

Staying calm and focused is one of the golden rules of refereeing

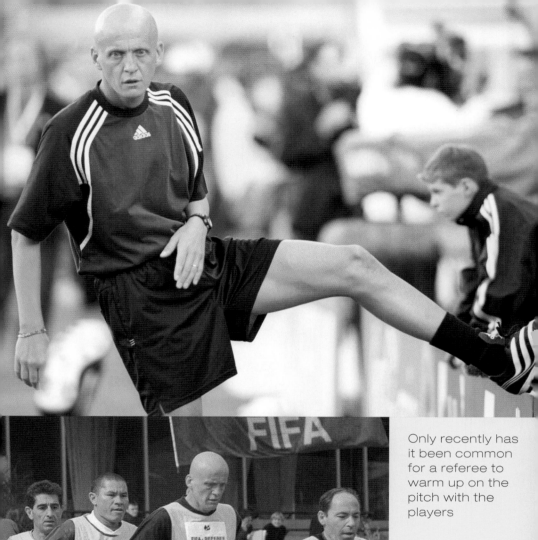

Only recently has it been common for a referee to warm up on the pitch with the players

Running the twelve minutes run outside Paris before the 1998 World Cup. From left: Esfandier Baharmast (USA), Lucien Bouchardeau (Nigeria), myself, Marc Batta (France)

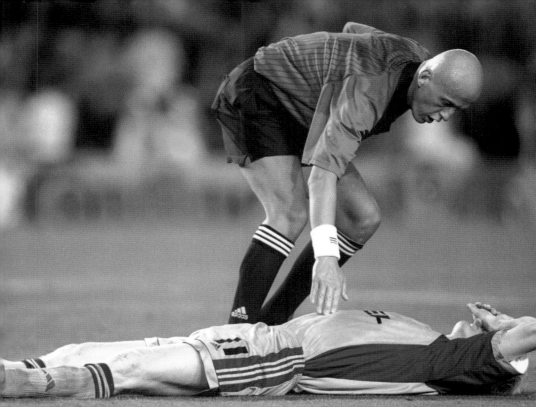

After the most exciting three minutes there has ever been in football, I offer my consolations to Stefan Effenberg

Walking in the rain: testing the pitch in one of the most controversial games of my career – at least if you are a Juventus supporter

Referees have a
sense of humour too:
with Gilles Veissiere
before Euro 2000

Receiving my trophy as
world's best referee 2000
from Franz Beckenbauer

I was still reeling from a bout of flu during the fitness test for the 2002 World Cup, but luckily was fit enough to attend. Here I am watching as Graham Poll and Anders Frisk try to keep warm

Showing David Beckham the penalty spot. Argentina–England was the one game I had been hoping to referee

My 'team' in the final. With (left to right) Leif Lindberg, Philip Sharp and Hugh Dallas

Below, left. The second, and final, yellow card of the World Cup Final steadied the game within the first ten minutes

Below, right. One of the finest moments of my career: breaking with protocol, FIFA President Mr Sepp Blatter placed my world cup medal around my neck just like one of the players

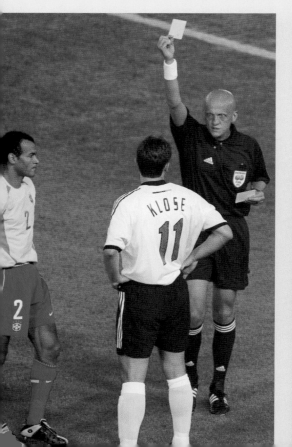

The shaking of hands before a game, I think, is very important – even though you might have just been talking to the same players moments before in the tunnel

I have never been afraid of intervening, even when tempers begin to fray

The flip-side to being a referee: wearing a Laura Biagiotti outfit during the *Donna Sotto le Stelle* fashion show in July 2002

Four

The Match

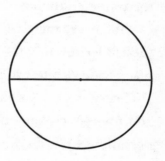

Seeing into the future

And so we're finally on the pitch. The match – ninety minutes, or just over – this is what all the preparation throughout the week has been building up to, all those hours spent out on the training ground.

And every match is a test, initially the games are rungs on the ladder towards the higher divisions and then, once you reach Serie A, a test to prove that you're up to it.

Every match is different, every match has its own story, and the referee has to be able to understand right from the beginning what kind of match it is. He has to be capable of picking up on the slightest nuance. In a word, he has to have a 'nose' for it.

Preparation helps you predict what might happen on the pitch, especially with regard to the teams' and the players' characteristics. It helps you develop a general plan for your approach to the game.

In all matches, and particularly in the most important, the first minutes are often the most decisive. Those very first decisions, the first blow of the whistle, these are the things that establish a sort of understanding with the players, which give the players the measure of the game. If you get those first decisions wrong it means the match might be uphill all the way for you, just as it is for a player who fluffs his first touch of the ball or his first few passes: such things can destroy peace of mind and confidence.

There is no one particular way of refereeing that works in all matches: the referee's skill lies in his ability to adapt his way of refereeing to the requirements of the match, or rather to what each moment of the match requires.

There are matches or moments in which the referee uses his whistle as little as possible, seeking not to interrupt the match too frequently and thus giving it fluidity and rhythm, because the behaviour of the players on the pitch allows him to do this. This is what is commonly called in Italy an 'English way of refereeing', because British players have an attitude that leads to them accepting physical contact on the pitch. In other games, or at certain moments, this sort of attitude can become extremely hazardous and in that case the referee has to be very careful and has to know how to change his own scale of values to adapt to events.

Let's take the Yokohama final as an example.

My team knew all there was to know about the technical and tactical characteristics of the two finalists. We were also aware that in such an important match the tension and the nervousness of the previous days and hours might cause some players problems, especially in the first minutes. The initial phase of the match was therefore crucial and if we managed to get it right then it would surely give us a good chance of achieving our own 'victory' in the final. And that's exactly how it went. There were two bookings in the first ten minutes for two spectacular fouls: the first one by the Brazilian Carlos Roque Junior, the second one by the German Miroslav Klose. It's not such a straightforward thing to start a World Cup final and find yourself with two players booked within the first ten minutes. What crosses your mind, and in all honesty this thought did cross mine, is, 'What if I've been a bit too rash? Perhaps it would have been better to give them a talking to and used the yellow card later on if necessary.'

But the right way is to be firm from the outset and then the players can relax into the game and unwind after all the tension of the build-up. You let them play, trying to intervene as little as possible, allowing the pace of the game to build up without too many interruptions thereby making the game as enjoyable as possible. The final result was that those two bookings remained the only two in a match that, for some observers, might have seemed an easy one to referee. If it was easy I have to say that it was thanks to those first ten minutes.

When I say that the referee has to have a good 'nose' what I mean is that a referee needs to be a good psychologist. He has to understand what's behind certain elements of the players' behaviour and attitudes, in order to work out in advance what might happen as the match develops. And being a good psychologist also helps in understanding certain reactions by players when they're on the pitch – for example when they don't agree with one of your decisions. A certain type of protest might even be acceptable because sometimes the tension resulting from the result's importance or from fatigue can mean that a player loses his cool. The important thing is that this doesn't create embarrassing situations for the referee, situations in which he loses face, because this can prove problematic for the remainder of the match.

And if the first minutes of the match are extremely important for the game, no less so are the last minutes – especially when the result is still open. Very often it's in these final minutes, sometimes in injury time, that the match-changing, even result-making incident materializes.

Unfortunately I have found myself on many occasions thinking, with just a few minutes to go, that the game has gone well, only to find a second later that something unforeseen has happened. I don't like to call this bad luck, because normally we all in some way make our own good or bad luck. The reason for this is therefore to be found in something more concrete, which might be the fact that the players' are more prone to making mistakes through fatigue. And tiredness can obviously affect the referee as well, meaning that he might have greater difficulty in making the right decisions.

The solution therefore lies in physical preparedness, in reaching the final minutes in the best possible physical state and knowing how to maintain maximum concentration and attention right up to the last second, even when you feel that everything has gone well and the match is firmly in your hands.

Together with the supporters of Manchester United and

Bayern Munich, I'll never forget the closing moments of the 1999 Champions' League final.

The game was played at Barcelona's Nou Camp stadium with over 90,000 supporters in a wonderful atmosphere. Bayern had gone 1–0 up with a goal by Mario Basler at the beginning of the first half and the match had progressed without any particular problems – the Germans were controlling play and the English team just couldn't manage to create any goal-scoring opportunities. Indeed, the Bayern strikers were really on form – hitting the post and the crossbar and forcing Peter Schmeichel, United's goalkeeper, to make some decisive saves. The German supporters were already celebrating what seemed like a win. Just a few seconds from the ninety-minute mark I let the fourth official, Fiorenzo Treossi, know that I intended to play three minutes injury time, or more precisely allowance for lost time.

Calculating this allowance included thirty seconds added for each substitution made, one minute for each injury requiring a stretcher on the pitch, and then any further time lost. At the forty-fifth minute of each half the fourth official signals the amount of injury time using an illuminated board.

On this occasion that signal marked the start of the three most incredible minutes I can remember in the history of football. Just twenty seconds into injury time Stefan Effenberg deflected a cross over the goal line, giving Manchester United a corner. Even Schmeichel was up there in the Bayern area in a desperate attempt to claw a goal back. The ball was cleared badly by a German defender and fell to Giggs who tried a shot from the edge of the penalty area that only found Sheringham whose deflection, unstoppable for Oliver Kahn, went into the corner of the goal.

While the English were celebrating, I went back to the centre circle thinking to myself, 'That's all we need . . . something's going to happen now and the match'll become a real mess.' The equalizer wasn't exactly great news for me as, up till that point, the game had gone smoothly with no contested decisions, no doubts and a scoreline that reflected the play – everything a referee could ask for. The equalizer meant extra time and so everything was open to discussion again because any debatable incident, any wrong decision would erase all the positive elements of the previous ninety minutes.

But the goal had been scored and all we could do was push on. The game got under way again and possession again fell to United. A fifty-metre pass to Solskjaer ended with another corner as he was tackled by Kuffour. Beckham set the ball down by the corner flag at forty-seven minutes and fifteen seconds – just forty-five seconds of play remaining. He lofted a high ball into the centre which Sheringham headed goalward and Solskjaer, no more than two metres from the goal line, stabbed the ball home – 2–1.

I'm sure no one who was present that night at the Nou Camp will ever forget the eruption of the English fans – a tremendous roar. And then the players' faces: sheer joy for Manchester United, complete shock for the Bayern team, their eyes empty and glazed as they struggled to accept that in the space of two minutes they'd seen victory vanish before their eyes. Many of them simply stretched out on the pitch, emptied of all physical and psychological strength. But there were still ten seconds or so left, and, as Freddie Mercury sang, 'The Show Must Go On'. So I went over to Effenberg who was lying on the ground and patted him on the chest, then I set about lifting the tearful Kuffour up off the ground and eventually we got going again.

A matter of seconds later I blew the final whistle, and once again the same scenes – the English celebrating and running around mad with joy, the Germans in tears, some on their knees, others with their faces in the grass.

Who could have imagined a climax like that just a few minutes previously? But that's football – from joy to despair in the blink of an eye. It was enough to make a normal sort of match something approaching the final of the century.

When seeing into the future is impossible

But sometimes, no matter how well you've prepared, situations that you could never have foreseen develop on the pitch. And precisely because you haven't imagined them, and because you haven't had to face them before, you might easily find yourself being unable to make use of your experience, all that baggage that each of us carries around and into which we delve for help in resolving the situations that crop up in life as they do on the football pitch.

But it's obvious why it's different to daily life: a careful person, a wise person, when faced with an unexpected situation says, 'Hold on, I'll think about this for a minute. I'll mull it over and then I'll decide.' When a lawyer finds himself being asked a tricky question by a client he has the possibility, or rather the duty if he's a real professional, of saying, 'I'll see you in a week's time, let me consider this.' A doctor can ask for further analysis before deciding on the best treatment. And even the figure the referee is most often compared to, the judge, before pronouncing his verdict, retires to his chambers to ponder, to evaluate, before making his decision.

We're not allowed any of this.

What we're asked to do, even in the most unexpected, unforeseen of situations is to make a decision in what's called 'real time', i.e. in a fraction of a second. This is not a simple matter.

I wish this enormous difference were understood by those who sit in an armchair in front of a screen, and after having seen the images several times, perhaps even in slow motion, say, 'Referees are like judges, they shouldn't make mistakes' – a comment I happened to hear recently.

In actual fact in certain particularly unusual situations, there is a bit of time available. In some cases you have to wait for something to happen and during that time, which can sometimes be relatively long, the referee has a chance to evaluate, to reflect, to seek a solution.

The fact that I'm a referee with a long career behind me

grants me, if for none other than statistical reasons, a wealth of experience of 'strange' situations.

One of these appeared in 1997 during an Inter Milan–Juventus match, one of the most important in the Italian league and a key event that season as they were the two teams at the top of Serie A. The San Siro stadium was completely sold out as usual and I can tell you that when there are more than 80,000 people at Meazza, things aren't easy for anyone – players and referees alike. You feel almost crushed by this wall of people looming over you and the roar is something truly breathtaking. After just seven or eight minutes the unusual incident took place. Two players, Paolo Montero of Juventus and Ivan Zamorano of Inter, jumped to head a high ball. The ball flew off towards the Juventus area and Maurizio Ganz, then playing for Inter, headed towards the Juventus goal from a position that was possibly offside. I looked to the assistant who gestured clearly to indicate that the ball was good and play could continue. As everyone knows, the assistants' role on the offside rule is crucial – if the referee isn't absolutely sure of the situation he has to rely on them. Not being in line with the penultimate defender, nor having the entire line of attack or defence at the centre of your line of sight can mean the referee isn't always able to see the position correctly.

My view was such that I really wasn't sure whether Ganz was offside or not, a blind spot, an area of the pitch that was out of my line of sight where there may well have been a defender, obliged me to accept my assistant's decision: he was certainly better able to see than I was. So the move continued

– Ganz's shot was saved by Angelo Peruzzi, but the ball came back to his feet and this time he scored. I gave the goal and the Inter players protested, not so much at me as at the linesman. My concern, at this point, was to defend the assistant from the players' protests. In situations like this the worst thing a referee can do is to abandon his assistant without helping him. I went over and tried to move Ciro Ferrara away, the Juventus player who was complaining most. When I was on the spot I heard the assistant respond to a question from Ferrara, 'No, he wasn't offside because the ball was played by Montero.'

A player who's in an offside position cannot be penalized if the ball is played to him by an opponent and therefore, if Juventus's Montero really had played the ball last, then Ganz would have been onside. But I was certain that the ball had been headed forward by Inter's Zamorano. I may have had doubts about whether a Juventus player had played Ganz onside, but I had no doubts that Zamorano had headed the ball. At this point I had to clarify immediately what had happened.

I asked the assistant, 'But was Ganz in an offside position?'

'Yes,' he replied, 'Ganz was offside, but the ball was played to him by Montero.'

To sum up the situation – the goal had been given, the scoring team had celebrated and the ball was already on the centre spot ready for the game to restart, yet now it was certain that the goal wasn't valid because Ganz had been offside and it had to be disallowed.

What had to be done was simple: a referee's main objective is to apply the rules correctly, and basing my actions on rule five, which says that the referee can change his own decision as long as the game hasn't restarted, I decided to change my mind and disallow the goal. What was going to be more difficult to manage were the repercussions. I was aware of the fact that an already delicate match could now become extremely difficult if my decision wasn't understood by as many people as possible. For this reason I called the Inter captain, Beppe Bergomi, over to me and said, 'This will seem strange, and you probably won't believe me, but you must trust me. Ganz was offside.'

I still remember the disbelief of the players, but once I'd informed them all of my decision, I had to do the same thing with the bench – the manager and the substitutes – because very often it's the bench that transmits agitation to the players on the pitch. I went over to the Inter dugout and had to bend down on one knee as Roy Hodgson, the Inter manager, was at least one metre below the level of the pitch. That way I could speak to him face to face. The photograph of me on bended knee before Hodgson must have travelled all over the world, but what was more important was the sporting gesture of the Inter manager, a true gentleman on and off the pitch. He shook my hand and said simply, 'That's all right.'

The first half continued as though nothing had happened. During the break the tension in our dressing room was particularly high because the decision and the process leading to it had clearly been very much out of the ordinary. Aside from this, the decision had been taken on the basis of something that had lasted a fraction of a second and that was difficult to see, so there was still a little voice in a corner of my mind saying, 'What if he was right?' But as we went back onto the pitch for the second half, Nicola Berti, who wasn't playing that day, came up to me and said, 'We've seen it on television. You were perfectly right.'

That was a confidence boost because yes, you have your certainties out there on the pitch, but you take on a heavy responsibility and Berti's gesture helped give me peace of mind. The match ended well – a 0–0 draw – and the episode that could have coloured the whole game remained no more than an isolated incident.

In order to reduce the risk that the incident might be interpreted wrongly and having consulted the representative of the Referees' Committee, I decided to appear in the press room after the match, something that is usually strictly forbidden for the referee. I remember trying to take on the role of captain of a team; I said, 'we made a mistake', 'we changed our decision', so as not to lumber all responsibility on the shoulders of the one member of my team who'd made the mistake. Unfortunately all this wasn't enough and over the following days there was a lot of fuss in the newspapers, with various opinions expressed. All this caused problems not so much for me as for a hotel in Playa de las Americas, in Tenerife. I'd had a family holiday planned for some time and we set off on schedule the day after the match. I'd asked a friend to keep me informed on a daily basis of the press coverage. I hadn't imagined that every day I'd be receiving metres and metres of faxes and the faces of the hotel staff who had no idea what was going on really were a picture.

And still today there are those who in recalling that incident, rather than talking of a terrible mistake having been avoided, choose to remember it as involving an extremely dubious decision by the referee.

Bending the rules

Despite the difficulties of a situation like this, the fact that the rules in some way make provision for such eventualities helps a lot. But sometimes even this isn't enough and then there's no preparation that can provide a magic cure for the referee – all he can do is turn to his common sense and his capacity for reflection. With regard to this I'd like to mention another incident which dates back to the 1999–2000 season. We were at the end of the Serie B championship and I was refereeing Foggia–Bari, a heartfelt derby that often, unfortunately, produces a variety of crowd troubles. This match was no exception, and during the first half there had been a series of unpleasant incidents. Supporters from both teams, taking advantage of the proximity of the terraces to the touch lines, had thrown objects onto the pitch. Fortunately the throwing had been limited by the fact the goalkeepers were playing below the areas occupied by their own supporters. Then at the beginning of the second half the two teams switched ends and the goalkeepers found themselves playing below the opposing supporters and all hell broke loose – despite the players themselves behaving in an exemplary fashion. I think only goalkeepers and assistant referees really know how difficult it is to stay on the pitch when you have your back turned to people who are throwing missiles that can potentially cause you serious injury. Your physical safety is truly left to chance because you have no way of protecting yourself, you can't avoid something that you can't see coming. Just consider what happens at some pitches in the minor leagues, where the assistants stand less than a metre from the supporters and throughout the match are subjected to a rain of objects, spit and even other fluids. This might make you smile, but it really ought to make you think. One assistant told me that on one occasion, on one of these pitches where the crowd are really close to the sidelines, a supporter kept trying to stab him with an umbrella.

I am convinced that the physical safety of anyone who's out on the pitch has to be safeguarded. I believe this to be a condition *sine qua non*; to put people's lives or dignity at risk for a game of football is unthinkable. It's amazing sometimes that people don't realize that even a small coin, if thrown from on high and if it hits its target in the right way, can cause really serious damage. Not to mention a 1.5-litre plastic bottle of mineral water thrown from the second tier, aided by the force of gravity.

Literally all sorts were flying onto the pitch that day at Foggia. Forcing people to play in those conditions, putting their physical safety at risk, didn't seem right to me.

The rules left me with no option: if I felt the safety conditions weren't sufficient to continue with the match, then after waiting to see if the situation improved, I could do nothing else than suspend the game indefinitely. But that might have been like pouring petrol on the flames of the clash between the rival supporters. The only possible alternative was to remove the targets of the violence – the goalkeepers of the opposing teams – by using the same method applied on occasions with the assistants. When an assistant, because of a decision he's made, receives protests from the crowd to the point where his physical safety can no longer be guaranteed – objects being thrown for example – then the positions are reversed: the 'innocent' linesman takes the place of the 'guilty' one. It's a makeshift remedy that has often resulted in a match continuing with no further problems. And while at Foggia we didn't really have much hope of stopping the rain of missiles, one of my assistants, who'd probably witnessed such things in the past, said to me, 'What if we were to swap the teams round?' I thought it might be a solution: there were no atmospheric conditions that made playing in one direction any better than the other – no wind, no interference from the sun – so neither of the two teams would have gained any advantage from playing in one direction as opposed to the other. I spoke to the two captains, because it seemed right to involve them in such an unusual decision that in effect meant bending the rules. They agreed with me on the two main objectives: protecting the players and continuing the game. Fortunately up to that moment no player had been hit and it was clear that the throwing depended purely on opposing players being near the supporters, therefore, moving the players would halt the rain of missiles. The teams rearranged themselves into their first-half positions, the game started again and the throwing, as predicted, stopped. Not everyone agreed with the remedy, but the seal of approval came from the top authorities: the president of FIFA and the sporting arbiter, who, when describing his motivation for validating the result, spoke of an interpretation that was *ultra legis* but *non contra legis*. Other commentators suggested instead that I shouldn't have bent the rules and should have simply suspended the match. I still feel, however, that if at all possible the objective of everyone who takes part in a match must be to try to bring it to its conclusion.

If one of the two goalkeepers had had the sun in his face or the wind had helped one team rather than the other, then it wouldn't have been fair and my decision would have been different. The same thing goes if one of the captains had told me he wasn't willing to continue. But everyone who was there at that moment agreed with the makeshift solution – a decision that proved to be the right one.

The rain man

The same logic of doing everything to make sure a match reaches its conclusion, informed my decision taken during Perugia–Juventus in May 2000, a game which later became famous. This too was an utterly extraordinary situation. It was the last day of the season and the weather was wonderful. It was such a sunny day that at half past nine that morning I'd been reading the newspaper outside at the hotel where I was staying with my assistants, up in the hills near Perugia, on Lake Trasimeno. The sun was so strong I had to look for shade after ten minutes. It was like a summer's day. At that moment the last of my worries was the possibility of bad weather. The clouds started coming in just as we were travelling to Perugia. Then, during the first half, it started raining, lightly at first and then increasingly hard. During half time the heavens opened. The pitch was unplayable and the easiest decision at that moment would have been to suspend the match.

Nevertheless, I was aware that just a few kilometres away from Perugia's ground the sun was shining and I knew that the surface of the Curi Stadium was among the finest in Italy in terms of drainage and capacity to absorb water. I'd already refereed a couple of times at Perugia with heavy rain and had seen that the pitch generally remained in good condition and that it drained and dried quickly after a downpour. The features of the playing surface, together with the fact that

I knew the downpour was in the finest cartoon tradition – it would disappear as quickly as it had arrived – made me decide to try to put off any final decision. I wanted to see first if the rain might stop and the pitch might dry up enough to allow the game to restart.

I tried a couple of tests using a ball and an umbrella, but the results were negative; though I remained convinced that the situation was improving as the rain was slackening off and some light was breaking through. Then, finally, after a decidedly long pause and a warm-up for the players, the second half got under way and the match was concluded.

Naturally, in this case, not everyone was of the same opinion, as is perhaps right. We can't all agree on everything. The thing I was pleased about was that all the neutrals who were present, particularly the pundits and the journalists, agreed with my 'let's wait and see' approach. At the end of the second half the playing surface was in no worse condition than the pitches on which many other games have been played.

The importance of the match, and the consequences of the final result for Juventus (they lost 1–0 and consequently only came second in Serie A, after having led the division for thirteen weeks), meant that those directly involved didn't agree with my decision. This is perfectly normal, I don't think there's anything strange about it. And still today when I meet a Juventus fan on the street, he's likely to remind me of the game that cost them the title and gave it to Lazio.

As is often the way, however, some people tried to look for an ulterior motive, suggesting that I was under pressure to make sure the match ended, pressure exerted by an entity often referred to as the *palazzo* – the seat of government in Rome, Lazio's city. I think it's truly sad to think that referees are looked upon as puppets whose strings are pulled by some higher force.

I don't mean to try to persuade anyone of the bona fide nature of my decisions, but I do want to defend the honesty and the decision-making independence of referees in general: we're certainly capable of making mistakes, but we do this on our own, with no one calling the shots.

Sometimes you make mistakes . . .

If what I've described up to now are all unforeseeable situations that hindsight shows I dealt with correctly, there are other decisions I've made that still leave me somewhat doubtful.

One of these was taken in Genoa, during a Sampdoria–Turin match. In this case it was a match that didn't seem to present any particular problems: neither the result nor the game itself gave rise to concerns over excessive reactions from the crowd. But at one point a banner appeared on the terraces with an offensive message aimed against the then head of the Referees' Committee, Paolo Casarin. It was something along the lines of 'Casarin is a clown', written in enormous letters. My immediate reaction was one of bemusement – I couldn't understand what this insult had to do with the match that was being played. There was no apparent reason for it, it seemed completely unnecessary. I decided it was my job to have the banner removed, since it appeared completely gratuitous. I spoke to the Sampdoria management and the captain, at that time Roberto Mancini. I tried to explain that it was worth intervening in some way to get the banner removed, that leaving it up there wasn't right. Whether they actually did do something still remains a mystery to me. Over the following days I read various reports in the newspapers. Someone wrote that Mancini went over to the crowd and told them, 'Don't take anything down.' I really don't know and I'm not interested in knowing. The banner was removed after a few minutes, only to reappear later. Whatever happened, I'm now sure that I didn't do the right thing. If I'd simply ignored it, it wouldn't have become an issue and probably would have been taken down anyway. By my actions I succeeded in giving it more importance than it warranted and I ended up, despite myself, giving the banner more attention and aggravating the situation through my mistaken decision.

A few months later, however, before a Piacenza–Milan game, a banner with an offensive message aimed at two of the players on the pitch appeared. Offensive, but above all else racist. In this case too I asked for the banner to be taken down, supported by the noisy reaction of the majority of the crowd in the stadium who started whistling as soon as it was unfurled. To have it taken down was the right decision, because in this case the offensive message wasn't aimed at any alleged sporting failure, but was directed at the dignity of the men involved, a below the belt blow at the principles of equality that are the foundation of sport and civil society.

Of course, in this case too I risked granting free publicity to an episode of incivility, but, when faced with certain abominations, the footballing world has to be able to take a stance, it cannot risk showing itself to be indifferent.

I don't believe that the stadium can become a sort of no man's land, a place where anything goes, where all types of behaviour are legitimate, or simply accepted because they are confined to a circumscribed place. There cannot be a sort of 'decriminalization' of a crime simply because it's committed inside a stadium. Once I heard a high-ranking police officer give a lecture in which he said that, all things considered, having certain types of people concentrated in the stadium made his job easier because they weren't wandering the streets committing other sorts of crimes. That made me shiver because that kind of attitude threatens to destroy football.

We have to look to other countries for examples, places where, when faced with serious problems regarding crowd behaviour at football games, difficult, repressive decisions have been taken, which have led to extremely positive results. France, for example, where simply throwing a firework is a criminal offence. Or, perhaps even more appropriately, England, for many years thought of as a place where violence in the stadiums was so endemic that UEFA was forced to exclude English clubs from the European cups. The introduction of well-enforced legislation – the Football Act of 1989, passed by Mrs Thatcher's government and then extended by Tony Blair's administration following Euro 2000 – has resulted in this situation being completely reversed in the space of a few years.

The results are there for everyone to see, all you have to do is look at the stands of any British stadium: parents with their children, families and couples out to enjoy themselves, to take part in the match, to spend a few hours watching the spectacle that is a football match. And all of them wearing the colours of their favourite team, without this carrying any risk for them. It's not that the English have all become angels, we know that when they travel abroad some of them still cause trouble, but it's not by chance that this happens in countries where the law is more tolerant, or where those who should apply the law don't do so in a consistent manner. And in any case, with regard to matches played abroad, those supporters recognized as being dangerous have their passports withdrawn. I'd like us here in Italy to achieve the same results. Up until recently, we were going in the right direction. However, the legislation that was introduced has been largely neglected, resulting in the problem returning with all its severity. Fortunately in recent months things have changed again and those who commit certain acts in the stadium can now be arrested later, following identification, without them having to be caught 'red handed'.

Why is it that we continue to see scenes broadcast on television of clashes between the police and supporters – hooligans is obviously a better word – who, their faces clearly visible, charge and attack the police with belts or sticks? And why is it that once they're identified, their only punishment is an order preventing them from entering a stadium for a certain period of time? In England, those who perpetrate certain crimes pay in a different sort of way – inside many English stadiums there are real cells.

I remember one of the first matches I refereed abroad. I was in Newcastle, England, and the security chiefs showed me the closed circuit television system they used. Every seat in the stadium was occupied by season-ticket holders and if any missile was thrown from any particular sector, an attempt was made first of all to identify the culprit and then his season-ticket was taken from him. If this proved impossible, the season-ticket was withdrawn from the entire sector under investigation. It's a system that might appear unfair, but it does involve those not responsible by putting responsibility on their shoulders, obliging them to work actively to identify the person who threw the missile.

When I'm refereeing a match and I have to call in the ground staff to clear the pitch of bottles, coins and oranges that have rained down from the terraces, I feel bad. 'We're here to try to let people enjoy themselves,' I say to myself, 'and the result is that all this stuff gets thrown at us.' There's no justification for it. When an action can cause physical injury to someone, not to mention the personal injury that a racist insult can cause, there cannot be any emotional or psychological explanation to justify it. And I'm sorry to have to say it, but in the short term only stiff measures can obtain results.

However, the measures required for improving the situation in the short term have to be supported by action that provides a sporting culture for those who go to the stadium – and this begins with the schools. It's important to make people understand that going to the stadium means going to see a show, to support your favourite team. Supporting should be about being 'for' a team and not 'against' another, which is what happens in countries where there is a more developed sporting culture. If we could achieve this in Italy then we'd have something that's normal in northern European countries and even in some with cultures similar to our own – Spain, for example – where there are no fences separating the crowd from the playing field.

I've often found myself warming up before a match in direct contact with the crowd. Sometimes there are corners between the advertising hoardings in the front rows through which it's possible to get onto the pitch, but this happens rarely and the only people who sometimes come out onto the pitch are those strange exhibitionists known as streakers who strip off and run naked just to get some attention and enjoy a few minutes as celebrities.

Five

The Referee's World

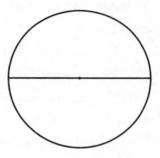

Why do you want to do that?

There's a recurring question that I'm asked by people I meet: 'But what made you want to become a football referee? What is it that makes a young lad become a referee?' It's not an easy question and it's difficult for me to come up with a suitable answer.

The instinctive reply is simply 'chance'.

The classmate who used to sit next to me at secondary school said one day, 'Why don't we sign up for a football referees' course?'

And I replied, 'Why not?'

It really was as simple as that.

But deep down I also think it's down to a great love for football, a desire to live football directly, to continue living it even though you've realized that your skills and technical ability will never allow you to have a future as a footballer.

It's this passion for football that drives those who decide one day to go to the referees' association in one of the many Italian cities and fill out the application form for a course. Perhaps at the beginning you think the passion might be satisfied simply by having a free pass for the stadium, so you get to go and see your favourite team's matches. Of course, this is a real incentive and many youngsters are obviously attracted by it, but this soon proves to be a minor detail and you find yourself continuing to be a referee for the simple reason that you like it, you enjoy going out onto the pitch with a whistle in your mouth.

Life at the local level

Few people are aware that behind each referee there's a large, organized movement. The Associazione Italiana Arbitri (Italian Referees' Association) has over 35,000 members and of those there are more than 24,000 who actually go out onto the pitches as referees or assistants. The remaining 11,000 or so are involved in education and training throughout Italy's local branches. There are many branches of AIA – 212 to be precise – and each of them is organized as a sort of club where the members, the referees, are able to meet, to talk, to spend an evening together.

I have spent many evenings in the premises of the Bologna branch, which was then in the city centre, together with colleagues my age and more senior referees. These were important times because we could recount our experiences and exchange opinions, which was useful for training and development, especially for the younger referees. It's not only out on the pitch that one learns and improves, but also in absorbing other people's experiences. This kind of training means that, rather than seeing certain situations out on the pitch, you see them in your mind.

By hosting referees' informal meetings, the branch transforms itself into a club and becomes something more than the place where the technical meetings take place – the meetings in which we talk and discuss the rules, analyse various interpretations and consider technical aspects of the game. Aside from these official meetings, almost all of the branches have recreational activities, from card games to dinners – all of which brings cohesion to the group and gives each referee a sense of being part of a larger society.

And now, years later, I can confirm that many of the friendships born back then in the branch, continue today. The branch I was born in, born as a referee that is, was in Bologna and, as branches go, it is very much at the forefront. They've always tried to give their members something extra. With this in mind a decision was taken to 'build', quite literally, new premises in an old agricultural machinery store granted by Bologna City Council. The labourers who worked on it were the referees themselves. Today, some twenty years later, the Bologna branch has spacious premises, able to seat over 200 people for meetings and at the same time host sports activities such as five-a-side football, basketball and volleyball. Not to mention the inevitable feasts, typical of Bologna's culinary tradition – tagliatelle with meat sauce and fried *crescentine*, a sort of dumpling.

Learning to be a referee

Whatever the reasons that lead you to want to be a referee, the next step is to register for one of the courses organized by the association. In recent years much attention has been paid to recruitment for these courses, especially because the number of teams that take part in the championship has grown. It may seem strange, but it's not easy to find enough referees to cover all the matches, which clearly poses organizational problems. The Italian Referees' Association, through its individual branches, has invested a lot of energy in its promotional work. Among other things there are school visits with support from quite famous names, for example Serie A referees who recount their experiences to those who are tomorrow's potential referees.

The would-be referees have to do an aptitude test for refereeing and following their application they undergo a series of medical check-ups and an athletic test. The prerequisites for registration are that you must be between fifteen and thirty-five years of age, and have good eyesight. Today sight problems can easily be corrected with contact lenses which don't interfere in any way with refereeing, but, in my day, lenses and spectacles weren't allowed. Consequently my classmate who'd had the initial idea of registering on the course found himself rejected because he wore glasses. Such is the irony of fate.

Once you're accepted, you take a technical course, held by

the instructors of the Italian Referees' Association, the primary objective of which is to teach the students the rules of football. Rules that are often mistakenly thought to be elementary and known by everyone. There are many sides to it all, many nuances in interpretation, so the rules are much more sophisticated than people usually think. Often those who've played football or have watched it from the stands or in front of the television are surprised by this.

I've been invited several times to give lessons to aspiring referees, almost always to speak not about the rules, but rather about their future career. On these occasions I've always met enthusiastic youngsters, keen to get going and with that same enthusiasm and drive that I had twenty-five years ago.

The preparatory phase lasts several months and at the end of it there's an exam, with a written and oral examination, in which the candidate is asked a series of questions. Those who pass are qualified to referee football games.

Novice referees

With the theoretical part over, the pitch lies waiting for you and you're appointed to your debut, your first match.

Usually you're not much more than a kid and so you can imagine the reaction when faced with your first 'real' match. Mine was a bit of a special initiation because before refereeing my first match I'd just happened to find myself, quite by chance, working in a regional league match. One afternoon I'd gone with two assistants from my branch to a pitch in Ferrara Province, Argenta, if I remember correctly, and because the referee had failed to turn up due to problems with the trains, I was 'promoted' to assistant. So my career began not in the middle of the pitch, as a referee, but on the sideline, as a linesman, as they were called back then.

A common problem for all new referees is the difficulty of using a whistle to signal an infringement of the rules. The process of seeing some action then reacting with a whistle is not as natural as it might seem. And sometimes, when you actually manage to whistle, the sound comes out in a manner that is frankly ridiculous: after all, you're running, you have this unfamiliar thing in your mouth, you have to blow into it and what comes out is a sound that is quite unlike a whistle.

But apart from the ridiculous whistle, in order to avoid a referee finding himself completely alone on his debut, there is always a sort of mentor, an expert referee, or an ex-referee, who can give him advice and suggestions.

The mentor is very important because, during this phase, the referee is learning. Just as trainers who deal with bud ding players, mentors have to limit themselves to working as instructors, let the competitive aspect of the game take second place behind the educational side and dedicate themselves to their pupil's learning. This learning takes place during the week and is then put into practice during the match, which becomes an extremely useful sort of weekly examination.

In the youth leagues, the role of the player who's learning how to play and the role of the referee who's learning how to referee ought to be clear to everyone. Unfortunately, however, many people do not recognize this and, very often, unfortunate incidents can take place among the onlookers. The spectators are usually relatives of those on the pitch and the incidents involve not only the referees, but the young players as well. The comments I've heard from some parents during those early days would warrant an entire book in themselves.

In any case this remains a period of growth that should be recognized as necessary for a young referee: the mistakes made on the field are what allow him to gain experience and it's thanks to the advice of those who have lived through all of this that he will be able to improve his performance.

For this reason I think the work carried out in the background by many ex-referees is very important. These are referees who perhaps haven't enjoyed particular success in the job, but who once they have been taken 'off the list' as we say in our jargon, continue to be members of the association and play a role as 'mentors'.

A mentor helps bring up the young referees not just when he goes to see matches, but also by spending time with them in the branches. To absorb others' experience through stories and the analysis of situations is extremely useful, as is doing so as an interested spectator. I say this from first-hand experience because when I was about seventeen or eighteen and I was just beginning to move into the world of refereeing, often, instead of going to see a match at the stadium in

Bologna, I would ask a referee from Serie D or the Promozione league, to go with him to his match. I was sure that witnessing a match at first hand, observing the behaviour of someone with more experience than I had, would accelerate my development. And in this way I saw a great number of minor matches, almost always passing up the opportunity of going with friends to see a Bologna match. But if I've learned to be a referee, I owe much to those matches I watched on provincial pitches.

Little referees grow

Another question I'm often asked is whether I started by refereeing kids' matches – as though a Serie A referee could start from any other kind of match. Naturally, the answer is yes – I started with a youngsters' match and right from the very beginning I had the good fortune to perform well enough to convince the then president of the Bologna branch, Piero Piani, to believe in my future in the upper divisions. And so it was that from the youth categories, with very young players who were still learning, I quickly went into the second category, skipping the 'dangerous' third category. Dangerous particularly for a young referee like me. This is the lowest category in Italian football, the one that any team can register in, and it leaves a lot to be desired – not just at the technical level, but also in terms of behaviour. The risk for referees doesn't really come from the crowd because there aren't usually many spectators, but more from the players themselves.

In just two years I was in the Promozione, the highest category of amateur regional football – in those days the Campionato di Eccellenza didn't yet exist.

In this period everything went very well and the only problem I actually had was on my debut in the Promozione. The match was to be played in Bellaria, a place on the sea in Rimini province. It was an important day for me and my parents, for the first and only time in my entire refereeing life, wanted to come and watch the match. Unfortunately it wasn't to be, as the Bellaria town council had been forced to close all the municipal facilities, including sports facilities, because of an outbreak of meningitis. Everyone had to go back home – you can imagine our disappointment.

My progress as a referee was just like everyone else, although perhaps it was more rapid than the average back in those days.

Back then, for a young referee like me, the traditional career path was rigorously adhered to. Even if someone proved to be particularly good, if he hadn't refereed a particular number of matches in the previous league and was a certain age, it was difficult, if not impossible, for him to move up into the next division. Today things have changed slightly and it's easier to overcome the age and number of game requirements – there are referees who reach Serie A at just twenty-eight years of age.

I think this is absolutely right, because if a person has the necessary talent and reaches maturity before others, it would be wrong to penalize him simply because of his date of birth.

I mention maturity because I believe this is one of the most important elements for a referee. Reaching a level of holistic balance, psychological and behavioural, the capacity to reflect and to interact with others calmly, is the winning card for obtaining results in any field, not just in refereeing. And it's acquiring these characteristics that is one of the most important things for a young lad who's starting out in the world of refereeing.

If you're the one who has to make the decisions and you're the youngest on the pitch, if you find yourself refereeing teams with players of twenty-seven or twenty-eight years of age and you're just eighteen or nineteen, in the First division or in the Promozione, where the managers are even older and the administrators might even be your parents, it's obvious that you need a maturity that goes beyond your years. The very role itself imposes these requirements. And if you have the opportunity and the good luck to be able to continue, the experience you gain will be indispensable. These positive elements are things that are useful in everyday life as well as in your working life. Knowing how to make a decision at a difficult time, under stressful conditions; knowing how to manage the people around you and who are depending on you; not letting yourself be affected by factors out of your control – these are all fundamental characteristics not just for a referee, but for many professional figures. This similarity with other walks of life means that I am often invited to professional training seminars to talk about my experience in sport.

Problems to be solved

Despite the many difficulties that a referee meets in the first years of his work, the satisfaction to be gained is such that the end result is almost certainly good.

To commit oneself to refereeing important matches, even at the youth or amateur levels, to referee matches between professional clubs in the Trainees category, or to referee a derby in the Promozione or Eccellenza leagues, these are all fantastic experiences that help show your abilities. Even at a personal level, such involvement brings with it a growth that is extremely valuable.

But there is the other side of the coin, for example the logistical difficulties involved in reaching the pitches where the matches are played. If you don't have a car you can't reach most of these venues because they are almost always in places not served by the train. This means you have to perhaps ask your father for help, who then has to take you there, thereby sacrificing his Sunday. Consequently, very often the young referee's enthusiasm has to be complemented by a parent's enthusiasm, a parent who might not be, as was my case, a football fan and so, because he or she isn't interested in what the people on the pitch are up to, ends up sitting in the car, reading the newspaper.

Logistical problems are often aggravated by crowd trouble and security problems.

I never tire of underlining just how remote this element is from (and must be kept from) the game itself. Football is a sport, football allows children and youngsters to be together, to socialize, to learn how to live together and achieve things together. Football is essentially a microcosm of life. In life you work with others to get results – in your office, with your group, for your company – just as you do in football. Rivalry and loyalty to one's team are part of football just as they are part of life, but it's madness to reach situations where the physical safety of players or referees is put in jeopardy. Unfortunately this happens, and sometimes youngsters who are sent to referee matches with players of their own age find aggravation not only on the pitch, but also from crowds of people insulting them – or worse. These people fail to truly understand why the people on the pitch are running after the ball. As players or as referees, these youngsters are not just playing, but they're learning values that will be indispensable to them in everyday life.

And if those players who want to reach the top accept these situations, stupidly, and see it as a price that has to be paid for their ambitions, they become unbearable for the no-longer young referees who get up early of a Sunday morning in order to let others play football.

I don't believe that delusions of grandeur or some kind of jealousy, reasons often given for a referee's motives, would lead a normal person to face such sacrifices. These are not the things that drive referees. They are motivated instead by a simple love for sport, love for what others do, because it's the others who play football. You may well enjoy yourself a bit as well, but you certainly help others' enjoyment much more than you satisfy your own. It really is sad to hear stories of violence or intolerance inflicted on referees at any level and I shiver when I hear, as happens in some divisions, that you only become a real referee when they've beaten you up. Luckily for me, over these past twenty-five years I've never been directly involved in particularly ugly or dangerous situations. Of course I have experienced moments at the end of matches when I've seen people come onto the pitch and run towards me, people who certainly didn't want to hug me and congratulate me on my performance. And I've also had to wait for a few hours in a dressing room while the situation outside defused sufficiently for me to be able to leave. Sometimes what happens around you is so unreal that when you look back on it years later, you can even smile about it.

I remember an incident when I was refereeing in Serie C, in a town in the Abruzzo region, Castel di Sangro. After the match a group of home supporters decided to wait for me outside the stadium with the intention, to put it mildly, of expressing their disagreement. After a while the carabinieri on duty decided to move us to their station, which, ironically, was just two hundred metres from the stadium, so that the 'besiegers', quite calmly, simply walked from the stadium to the police station. Fortunately, it being winter, the dark and the cold eventually convinced them that perhaps they'd be better off at home and so the siege was over without having to wait for reinforcements.

Perhaps it's normal for passion, for supporting a team, to lead people to identify the referee as a sort of enemy, especially if that referee on previous Sundays or in previous years has taken decisions that have in some way damaged your favourite team. Even the chants of insults don't really constitute a serious problem and I've never seen an insult cause any serious injury. The real problem is physical aggression. I don't believe threatening, antagonistic behaviour can be tolerated at any level. Certainly not at youth and amateur level, where the game should principally be about enjoyment – a way of engaging in sport seasoned with the pepper of competition. But even at the professional level, if you really want to look upon your team's opponents and the referee as enemies, you still owe them respect as men. To throw a coin or, worse, a bottle of water or a firework from the second tier of a stadium, without knowing where it might end up and without thinking that the action might cause serious injury to anyone who's hit, is utterly unbelievable. Many people will certainly remember what happened many years ago at the Olympic Stadium in Rome when a rocket hit a peaceful supporter on the terraces and killed him. More recently the same thing happened in the stadium in Messina. I do not believe there is any kind of support that justifies this.

If we are not capable of finding, once again, the values of tolerance and civil society, the future of football looks very dark. And unfortunately not just the future of football.

The erstwhile lads

There are referees who continue to work even though they have no hope of reaching the higher levels, even though their refereeing careers are already over. I call them the erstwhile lads because they're no longer of an age to be considered young, some of them are between thirty-five to thirty-eight, some of them older, but they still have all the keenness and the passion of lads. It is this great passion that drives them out in any weather and at any time on to some muddy pitch when they could quite easily stay in bed of a Sunday morning, or go to a bar for a quiet breakfast and read the newspaper.

One of the erstwhile lads is very close to me. His name is Pino Leiti, he's thirty-six years old, and was an assistant in Serie C. He was a great help to me when I was getting ready for Euro 2000 and the 2002 World Cup. At the end of the season, when he could have rested because his work had finished, he embarked on a month of extra training as my running partner. There's nothing worse than running alone, and when you have to push yourself it's crucial to have someone alongside to spur you on, someone who supports you in the moments when you feel run down. And so Pino, after having finished his work as assistant, started the season again by going to referee a youngsters' match in the Massa province with all the spirit and the pride of a man going to referee a Serie A match.

I have two daughters who don't play football, but if they should ever decide to take it up I'd be glad to know that they were being 'helped along' by a person like Pino, or one of the many others like him, who work on pitches throughout Italy. I would be happy and I have no words to express fully my respect and my gratitude.

For this reason I am truly saddened when I see that often in a beginners' match, where the average age is around ten, the referee receives an avalanche of insults because he's whistled or hasn't whistled for a penalty.

Nevertheless my hope, in my heart rather than in my head, is that this bad behaviour comes from a poor, if not totally non-existent, awareness of the values of those who referee. I would like to instigate meetings between those who play and those who referee, even at the youth level, to share their experiences and motives, their knowledge and ambitions. Out of a reciprocal awareness different views and behaviour would surely come about.

If something is done for the good of a young lad, then the last to complain about that ought to be his parents. But as this is not necessarily taken into account, I feel it would be worthwhile trying to make the role of the referee, at this level, clearer and more recognizable. Attempts are being made to do this, but there's still a lot of work to be done.

What is the referee's real role?

One evening, while we were sitting alongside each other in the stalls at the Ariston theatre in San Remo, both about to receive a prize, Edgar Davids, a man of few words, but a man whose words usually hit the mark, said to me, 'There's something I don't understand, when I go out onto the pitch, I go out to win, for me and for my team. But you? What do you go out there for?' Well, for me and for other referees like me, we go out onto the pitch to try and help the real competitors, the players, to play in full respect of the rules and therefore to play in the best possible way. Usually people play best when the rules are respected. The most spectacular games are those in which few fouls are committed, those in which the game isn't interrupted continually and the pace is kept at a high tempo. The referee is the person who helps the teams put on a show which, especially at the highest levels, is in the best possible shape so the 'footballing product' can please those who 'buy' it – those who go to watch it in the stadium, on television, those who talk about it and are passionate about it. I believe there is little or no enjoyment in watching players giving or receiving 'the treatment'. We can only really talk of a 'show' in those matches that are played at high pace and in which there are, at the most, about twenty-five interruptions in the match, corresponding to the same number of 'normal' fouls – those committed because the player arrives at the ball a fraction of a second late compared to his opponent. In those matches where there are, say, more than fifty-five fouls, it's inevitable that the sense of show declines drastically.

The referee's role is therefore one 'of service', a person who isn't on the pitch because he wants to decide things for himself. Neither is he there, as I hear suggested every now and then, to steer the match through to the 'right' result. The referee is there to let the players best display their abilities as footballers. To succeed in this, every referee has to always try to give his best, to try to make sure that he too, in his own way, wins.

As with every person who sets out to win, the referee, throughout the ninety minutes of a game, is his own best supporter. It makes me smile when someone asks me if I support a team. It makes me smile, but it also makes me realize just how little people know of referees and of their way of thinking. Obviously, every referee will have had, or will still have, his own favourite team. It's not as though we come from Mars – of course, in our childhood and adolescence football had an important role – so to think that a referee has never been a supporter is ridiculous. But it's significant that this question is always put to referees, never to the players, as though it were normal for them to support one team while playing for another. And in fact that's exactly how things are – there are players who are famous for being great supporters of one team and during their careers they have found themselves playing against that very team. For example, Walter Zenga, who was Inter Milan through and through, went on to become their goalkeeper, their captain and their symbol. When he went to play for Sampdoria no one ever thought that when he found himself playing against Inter Milan he might in some way do something to favour his favourite team. Players are professional and when they go out onto the pitch they only think about giving their all towards victory. Well, the same thing is true for referees. When I step onto the pitch my only objective is to give the best possible performance and the last thought in my mind is that one of the two teams out there with me might be my favourite. And just as Zenga tried to save everything that came at him during the matches against Inter Milan, while at the same time celebrating every other success of Inter Milan in the championship, the referee, when his ninety minutes are over, will celebrate the victories of his favourite teams. Rest assured, however, that during the match he is only a supporter of himself.

Referees who pay

Further proof of the depth of passion that drives referees is that they have always had to pay the expenses incurred in refereeing matches in advance and out of their own pockets.

By this I mean the cost of the journey, the meals and possibly the hotel. All this can mean fifty or so Euros for trips relatively near home, but can reach several hundred Euros for longer journeys. The referee pays for all this and is then reimbursed, usually some months later.

Not just grief

In compensation for the problems there are fortunately many pleasurable sides to refereeing.

Above all else there is the social element: working together with others who share the same enthusiasm, other referees from your branch or those who work in your league; sharing experiences, both good and bad; finding help at the most unexpected time and place from those who helped you many years before. I don't think I'm exaggerating when I say that the referee's world, as a social phenomenon, involves unity, solidarity, and openness with regard to colleagues. These are values that aren't easily come by in other circles and which, and I hope I'm not misunderstood here, make it sound similar to the Masons. This gets to the stage whereby you're prepared to offer any sort of help to people you don't even know, simply because they belong to AIA. I think there are very few associations in which there is a stronger sense of camaraderie.

Naturally, of course, there are also the pleasures that comes from your own personal achievements. A good perfor- mance, a positive match, being aware that you're doing a good job, these are all things that afford ample compensation for the sacrifices made. And this, I repeat, doesn't necessarily mean reaching the highest divisions.

Out of 25,000 referees working in Italy today, only thirty-five referee in Serie A and B, a percentage so low that in statistical terms it doesn't offer a great deal of hope of making it – it's closer to a one in a thousand chance.

The satisfaction obtained by referees from the so-called minor divisions, especially the youth leagues is much more important. Here, enjoyment comes from the knowledge that their efforts help other people to enjoy themselves through sport – particularly the young and the very young.

It's not easy to explain, and it's probably even more difficult to understand it, but I believe that this satisfaction is priceless, amazing and deeply personal. I don't want to liken the referee's job to some sort of volunteer work, but there's no doubt that there are many similarities between the refereeing and the voluntary worlds.

Youth sport is fundamental in bringing up a healthy generation with strong common values and it works towards making sure that we can engage in sport on a widespread scale. All this grants referees the deepest possible fulfilment that their work can possibly offer.

But, obviously, there's the satisfaction that comes from being good enough, and lucky enough, to move up through the divisions, to test yourself in championships that are increasingly important, where the level of play rises with the significance of the matches. For a career referee there is undoubtedly an element of competition. It's right that it should be this way. Sacrifices are made in trying to do a good job and if you do a good job then you reach certain levels. And since not everyone can make these sacrifices or reach those levels, there has to be a form of selection that is also based on competition.

The satisfaction of being at the top, of being considered one of the best, of consistently being among those selected for the various promotions through the divisions, is an undeniable satisfaction.

The bottom line

If I were to attempt to sum up my credit and debit sheet between negative experiences and positive achievements through my twenty-five years as a referee, I'd say that the positive achievements clearly outweigh the many difficulties I have experienced.

Certainly today satisfaction prevails, even though there are moments when the question, 'What am I doing this for?' runs through my mind, particularly when things go wrong. It's then that I realize that, despite all the efforts to prepare in the best possible way, I'm savagely criticized just because the replay shows something that I could never have seen. In those cases the temptation is to just let them get on with it: you want television? Then you can keep it . . .

In general those lucky enough to reach the levels I've reached do draw enormous satisfaction from their work, satisfaction that's difficult to describe and explain. The chance to be part of the world of the great champions, to watch them in action, participate in a match with them, is something fantastic – and this comes from a man who collected football stickers right up until he went to university.

Nevertheless, I'm not sure that if I hadn't achieved what I have over these past years then I wouldn't have continued to referee at the lower levels. There is of course no proof of this. What I can say is that the last game I refereed before setting off for the World Cup in Japan was a trainee league match in Livorno.

I enjoy what I do, and to be able to do it I've made sacrifices. Or rather, I've made choices, particularly professionally, that have given me the time and the ability to be a referee. Certainly, if I hadn't concentrated on refereeing, my professional life would have taken me along a different road. For example, I may well have found that I didn't have the time, rather than the inclination, to continue refereeing, even at lower levels.

My working life has all been geared to my wanting to be a referee and today I can say that I made the right decisions. I like what I do and the proof of this is that every time I'm left on the bench, every time I'm not appointed to a match, although I understand the need for a 'turnover' of referees, I certainly don't jump for joy.

Organizing refereeing

The organization of AIA is at the cutting edge in world terms because of the attention it pays to the less visible aspects of its work. Each branch has a President and a council of directors who look after the management of the local youth and amateur championships. The regional committees coordinate the work of the various divisions at local level and in turn are coordinated by the National Committee. These various organs manage both technical and association activity by means of a series of commissions that follow the various championships and supervise the growth and the selection of referees for their promotion from one division to another, relying on the judgement provided by observers.

Career referees

A referee starts his work in the youth leagues and is monitored by observers, who report back to the commission. On the basis of these reports the committee decide whether to put him forward for promotion. The observers' reports are never of the simple 'good' or 'bad' type. Post-match analysis plays an important role in a referee's development – the observer goes to the dressing room and discusses the match and what he has seen. This conversation, if it is approached positively, and involves constructive criticism, is of great value in improving a referee's performance. And it's a system that works at the highest levels too – in both Serie A and in international matches – even though for the more expert of referees it ends up being principally a sort of check-up on your form and how you interpreted the match. As I mentioned, the observers' reports are read by the commissions and are the instruments used for the selection of referees, a selection that becomes progressively more demanding as you move up through the divisions. Just consider that from the approximately eighty referees in Serie C, only four at the end of the season will be promoted to Serie B. Only 5 per cent, evidence of just how difficult it is to make it.

As you can see, this is a careful, strict and very rigorous form of selection. It's only normal that mistakes can be made, however. Perhaps some good referees are lost along the way, but I'm convinced that if this does happen then it's more likely it happens through the referee's own fault rather than by any fault on the part of those who evaluated his performance. If you have all the necessary talent then you make progress. You might waste a year or so, but sooner or later you'll manage it.

The referee's profession

Among all the various things that a referee can achieve through his work, it's impossible not to turn our attention to the matter of money. This may only concern referees in the professional Serie A and B in Italy, but it's nonetheless important to consider it.

The Federazione Italiana Giuoco Calcio (Italian Football Federation) and the Italian Referees' Association understand that in order to provide what professional football needs, referees have to be able to dedicate time and energy to their preparation. An obvious consequence of this is that they have to take time out from their usual activities. Refereeing can therefore no longer be carried out just as a hobby. In any case, for me, a hobby means simply a pastime, something done as a distraction, for relaxation. A hobby might be going fishing, playing golf, going sailing, certainly not refereeing a Serie A match. And if I were director of a club or a player or a manager, I wouldn't be happy to think that the person who plays such an important role in a match is doing it just as a pastime.

In order to make sure that referees have all the necessary time, the Italian federation, in conjunction with FIFA and UEFA, decided to give them a salary, something that for a large-scale outfit like the Italian association is easier than it would be in countries where football doesn't have the same economic importance.

Referees' salaries have increased with the amount of involvement that's now expected of us.

Phase one in this process was initiated at the end of the 1980s, and was followed by phase two, which began four years ago at the same time as the training camps. These were held every week in the first year and in the second year bi-weekly.

With the residential camps, the compulsory training during the week and all the preparation and the time required to make ourselves available to the Federation, a remunerative system was brought in, based partly on an annual bonus and a payment for each match refereed. Match payments differ according to whether the match is in Serie A, Serie B or in the Italian Cup. Compared to average salaries in Italian companies, a referee who often works in Serie A has a medium-to-high salary, which sounds significant until you compare it to the average of the incomes in the context in which we work – the world of football.

To place all of this in perspective, however, we have to consider the practicalities of the life referees lead. Nowadays refereeing football matches at the professional level means having to make very important professional choices, sometimes radical choices, because very often your day job doesn't fit easily around refereeing. Therefore many of us have found ourselves forced to choose work that's different from what we'd been involved in previously – for example insurance, financial consultancy, or associates in a legal practice. The number of referees who work as employees is decreasing all the time and those who continue in such work are only able to do so because of particular agreements reached with their employers.

In some cases the popularity you achieve can be a help, but the fact that you can't dedicate the necessary time to refereeing is a serious drawback. This is especially true in the crucial period between thirty and forty-five years of age, when the most important stages of your working life coincides with refereeing at the highest levels. Similarly, if a referee stops officiating at forty-five years of age, after ten or eleven years in Serie A, it's unlikely that he'll be at the same level as those full-time colleagues who during the same ten or eleven years have gained more experience in their chosen profession.

An economic evaluation, therefore, should not be made only in terms of the remuneration for the time someone spends as a referee. It should also act as an indemnity, a compensation for the things we will miss out on in the future because we haven't been able to lay a professional foundation in the present.

The most important thing is that, in one way or another, everyone understands that in order to carry out his work a referee needs time to dedicate to his preparation. We no longer have referees who work throughout the week, training twice at seven in the evening, and then go off to referee of a Sunday. Today all it takes is a week in which you train less well than you usually do, perhaps because you've had a touch of flu, and you really feel it when you're out there on the pitch. You might manage to do a good job just the same, but at kick-off you know you won't feel 100 per cent.

In the same way that football players do all they can to get out on the pitch before they give in to an injury or a bout of flu, I do the same because relinquishing a match is something nobody likes to do. Fortunately my system reacts well to treatment and, aware of this, I know that if, for example, I come down with flu even just a few days before a match, it doesn't cause me any problems. I can count then on the help of the Serie A referees' doctor, Angelo Pizzi, who's from Viareggio like me and who has more than once been called upon to get me back on my feet in record time.

So what, then, is the difference between a Serie A referee and a football professional? It's a very subtle one, to tell the truth, and perhaps it's really only a question of formal status. An international referee who works abroad during the week and in Italy at the weekend, can't have much time to dedicate to other work. Consider that over the course of a season there are twenty-five, three-day training periods at Coverciano, one eleven-day camp at Sportilia, an average of twenty-five championship matches, each requiring two days' work, and so we reach some 130 days to which you have to add, for an international referee like me, some ten or so international matches, each involving three days away. This means the total of the days spent away from home each season reaches 160. If we then take into account the compulsory training, there's not much time left for your own work.

The future lies in an increasing professionalization of the referee's job. I don't think we can even consider reversing this tendency. The need for ever-better preparation produces the need for professional referees. But we have to be careful because the idea that a well-paid professional referee equals a referee who never makes mistakes does not work. Being professional means achieving the best possible conditions for doing one's job, training to the best of one's abilities with the awareness that despite everything a mistake may well be made.

I don't know if the formal status of the professional referee will be recognized, but the most important thing is that we are able to behave like professionals and that all football organizations understand the need to invest in referees. But we have to be careful to not just devote this to elite referees, or just to today's referees. We have to invest in the future and create referees of tomorrow. Attention therefore has to be paid to the youngsters as well, just like football clubs do with their academies of excellence where future champions grow.

Six

My Own World

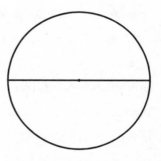

A footballing child

It feels a bit strange to start a new chapter of the book, a chapter dedicated to my own story and my private life, with a 'traditional' formula, but I can't think of a better way to get started. So here it is.

I was born in Bologna on 13 February 1960, under the sign of Aquarius. My parents are both from the province of Bologna: my mother was born on the Romagna border, in Imola, while my father was born on the Apennine hills between Bologna and Modena. For many years my mother was a primary school teacher, while my father worked as a clerk for the Ministry of Defence. Because they both worked, I spent a lot of time with 'Nanny Bice', an old lady who looked after me, before going to nursery school. Right from that early age I preferred pasta to meat and Nanny Bice always made sure I ate my meat before my pasta.

Even though I was born in February, my parents decided to send me to school – a private school run by nuns – a year early, at five and a half. Back in those days you couldn't do the first year of primary school at the age of five, not even in the authorized private schools like the Sisters of Saint Anna School in Bologna.

So I became an 'illegal' pupil and when the school inspectors came, the nuns used to hide me, which I wasn't too happy about.

Then, once I'd passed the first-year exam as an external candidate, I moved into the second year as a fully registered and official pupil.

The memories I have of those years are somewhat confused, but there are some very clear flashes. For example, I remember very well the way one certain nun used to pinch your cheek or pull your ears when you did something wrong and how we were all terrified of her.

Then there was one day when for lunch I was forced to eat a cabbage-based dish that my mother had prepared in the little 'tin' that all the children took to school. Still now whenever I smell cabbage I run a mile.

And then there was the day, in the first year of primary school, when the director arrived and they hid me in a storeroom in the part of the building where the nuns lived, leaving me to spend the whole morning there.

Less vague, however, are my memories of the never-ending games of football played on what was called 'the little pitch', a place behind the parish church where two sets of goalposts had been set up. The pitch was literally a stone's throw from home and when the weather was good we played all afternoon, until dark.

I would get back home completely drenched with sweat and my mother regularly gave me a good shouting at, particularly if I ended up with a cold. Some years later we discovered that those colds were really an allergy and a series of other things that had nothing to do with sweating, but I was shouted at anyway.

Such was the depth of my attachment to the little pitch that when we moved home – I must have been about nine years old – and we went to live no more than 800 metres from the previous house, for me it was like moving from one city to another. Fortunately, as is always the case, the unease didn't last long – just the time it took to find 'a new little pitch', perhaps even better than the old one, and some new friends. Actually, the change became an advantage because this way with two groups of friends the matches became even more exciting.

Football was the order of the day even when the pitch was unplayable because of too much rain, snow or cold. Then the matches shifted indoors and were played on the floor, with two goals made of Lego and a series of teams using football cards. It was like a sort of home-made Subbuteo with a tin-foil ball and a reinforced goalkeeper so that he wouldn't be flattened with every shot.

We used to organize Italian-style tournaments with home and away legs. Quite literally home and away, so that you had the difficulty of getting used to playing surfaces, or rather tiled floors, that were different from the one you were most used to.

Each of us chose our own players on a transfer market basis that perhaps had more to do with our own personal likes and dislikes than with the real fame and skill of the players. I remember for example that the strong point of my team was the then centre-forward of Napoli, Umile, who passed away at an early age some years ago and who certainly scored more goals in our tournaments than he ever did in Serie A.

The passage from primary school to middle school wasn't easy at first. My parents chose a school for me in the city centre, while all my friends went to a school not far from home, and so I felt a little cut out of their interests and the things that were happening in their lives. On the other hand, in this way I had the chance to meet boys and girls from other areas of the city and in the long run this proved to be a good thing.

Then there were the excellent pizzas from what is still one of the most popular sliced-pizza pizzerias in Bologna – Altero in Via Ugo Bassi. I often ate a slice before going into school in the morning, another as a snack at playtime and yet another before going back home.

Then I enrolled at a scientific secondary school, one of the most well established in Bologna – the Righi. Here too, no particular problems: I got through all my subjects each year, except for once, in the third year of the *liceo* when I had to repeat Italian after failing the written exam.

My Italian teacher, a well-known figure throughout the school, had some very radical ideas and was close to being extreme left-wing. My ideas were diametrically opposed to hers. I still remember a comment she wrote on one of my class tests, a composition in which we had to write about how we would solve the problem of delinquency: 'smacks of the truncheon and castor oil'. I got four out of ten for that.

From that point on I realized that it was always better to choose the literature questions. Unfortunately, though, for that year the damage was done and so I ended up spending the summer studying Italian literature and writing essays.

Studying wasn't exactly among my priorities at secondary school and during lessons, with those teachers who let us do it, it was much more enjoyable to hang around in the corridors and chat. On Saturday mornings there was the ritual of live World Cup skiing on the portable television that belonged to one of my friends; this took place in an empty classroom whose occupants at that moment were in the gym for physical education.

In accordance with the motto 'maximum yield with minimum effort', I reached my *maturità* exam, the equivalent of A levels. To everyone's surprise, not least my parents', I managed to get forty out of sixty – a mark decidedly better than expected.

And a studious adolescent

Registration at university was plagued by uncertainty. I spent the summer beforehand, well not quite all of it, trying to decide which degree course to take and right up to the deadline I wasn't sure whether it was to be economics or law. Both of them attracted me because of the type of study and because of the future possibilities they offered, but in the end, and on the very last day, I opted for economics. Who knows, perhaps if I could go back in time I'd register for law, which is something I did after my first degree. Some of the economics subjects were validated and I would have been able to get a law degree in reduced time, but I'd already started working and to tell the truth spending my evenings at home studying wasn't my main ambition at that time.

My five years at university – five because while I was there I did my year of military service – ended with a final mark of 110 out of 110 with distinction.

Those years were great fun and very intense, years that cemented all sorts of friendships that still last today.

Days at the university were spent between lectures and study in the faculty library, the 'Bigiavi' in Via Belle Arti. Perhaps the word study is a little bit exaggerated because in the end we spent most of our time on the videogames in the bar opposite or just chatting. We reached a sort of compromise: the library was on three floors and the first two became the place we would go to when we really had to study for an exam, while the ground floor became a meeting place for people who preferred to chat.

As mentioned above, at the age of twenty I decided to do my military service and I opted for the fire brigade. This wasn't because I had any particular interest in being a fireman, but rather because this way I was sure of being able to stay in my own city. I can't deny that some influence had to be used, as otherwise it would have been very difficult to get in. After a two-month course in Rome I was assigned to the Bologna province headquarters to the commander's secretarial team. This was quite a prestigious, sought-after job and there were occasional 'adventurous' outings on the engines with sirens blaring.

I had some problems with one of my knees in this period: a cartilage operation involving a period of convalescence that should have lasted until the end of the close season. But my passion for refereeing played a dirty trick on me. I was feeling quite well and I'd already started training again, so I thought the moment had come to start refereeing again, without thinking that this might cause problems. Unfortunately a report on a match I'd refereed came to the notice of one of the full-time firemen in my section and he decided to show it to the commander. To say that the commander didn't take it very well is to put it mildly. I received a telegram at home ordering me to report for a medical examination with the fire brigade's doctor, not the doctor in the military hospital who'd granted me the period of convalescence. The result of all this was that my convalescence was rescinded and I got a new job – I was moved from the administration to the kitchens, becoming an expert in potato peeling and earning a permanent position in the frontline team, those who go out first for all the calls. Fortunately all this happened just a few months before the end of my service, but I certainly made up for all the work I'd missed during my convalescence, and more besides.

Head the ball

Football has been a constant feature in my life. After the endless games on the little pitch when I was at primary school, I
started playing in the team of the local parish, the Orione. Perhaps I should say that I started sitting on the bench because
I didn't actually get to play all that much and I really felt the
frustration of hardly ever kicking the ball. Then, when I was
about fourteen, I got one up on the parish team. Together with
some friends I had a trial with another team and at the end of
the game I overheard a comment from a couple of guys: 'Perhaps we've found our sweeper.' This made me really happy
and for two years I was the regular sweeper for Pallavicini, one
of the most established teams in the Bologna youth section.

Then, after the last year in the youth team, came my classmate's fateful question: 'There's a course being organized for
referees, why don't we register on it?' And that was the start
of another story.

A supporter before being a referee

As well as playing football, like almost all Italian young
sters I also loved watching football from the terraces of the
stadium. A season ticket for our favourite team was the most

sought-after gift of the year and my first one for Bologna arrived when I was about ten years old. I used to go to the stadium with another boy my age and his father. The atmosphere back then was very different – it was light years away from the stadium today.

But rather than football, my past as a supporter had more to do with basketball, the sport which in Bologna creates greater rivalry because there are two teams in the city.

Unlike the vast majority of my friends, all of them keen supporters of Virtus, a rich and successful team, I chose Fortitudo as my favourite, which was then the poor team, the one that was continually on a roller coaster between the A and B division, between A1 and A2. Virtus were always winning championships and cups, while our only chance of ever getting our own back was when there was a derby, the only opportunity we had for some revenge.

Basketball – my first love

Only people who have lived in Bologna can understand what rivalry in basketball means, just as only those who were born in Siena can understand the real nature of the Palio. For people from elsewhere it might well be a great show, but only if you live it daily can you manage to appreciate it fully.

I have an inordinate amount of memories related to basketball, many players who had truly mythical status in my mind – Gary Schull, the famous Baron, Marcellous Starks, the ebony giant, and of course Carlton Myers, who was and still is one of the best Italian basketballers. Memories of so many matches, the tension that makes you sit through it all like a sort of suffering rather than enjoyment and then the bitterness at the defeats. The worst was the one in the Korac Cup final in Genoa, Fortitudo's first-ever final. It was against Jugoplastika, a team we probably would have been able to beat if a decision taken by the international Federation hadn't prevented us from playing one of our best men, the Italo-Argentine Carlos Raffaelli.

It's curious how basketball immediately captivated my wife as well, while she remains completely untouched by football. There was a period when I even 'used' her as a sort of good luck charm for the derby with Virtus: she managed to bring a string of eight consecutive derby victories for Fortitudo, to the point where some supporter friends and managers of Fortitudo, first and foremost Fabrizio Pungetti, public relations director, always asked me whether she was coming to the matches. On occasions when there was any danger she might not make it they pleaded with me to make sure she would come along.

An anecdote from 1996 explains the depth of my passion for Fortitudo. I was in China to referee the first friendly that a European team, England, had ever played there. Over the days following the football match I was to be involved in a series of meetings and lectures in Beijing, except that on the Saturday Fortitudo were playing against Stefanel Milano, the third-last match in the championship. Desperate, I managed to invent an excuse to bring forward my return to Italy by one day so as to be in Bologna on the Saturday afternoon, changing my flights from Alitalia to Air China. I got off the plane during a stopover in Milan, hired a car, and even though I shouldn't say it, let alone have done it, I drove from Malpensa to Bologna with my foot on the floor. All this to arrive just in time to witness a home defeat that cost us the championship.

The only meagre consolation came from a memorable feast of tagliatelle with meat sauce, ham *crescentine* and *squacquerone*, a very delicate cheese – a meal I treated myself to in an attempt to forget both the result and six days of Chinese cuisine . . .

Yes, the more I bring back to mind memories related to basketball, the more I realize that, while this sport is not perhaps capable of making me lose control, it certainly moves something deep inside of me. I remember a match between Pallacanestro Pistoia and Fortitudo, which I was invited to by the owner of a company called Madigan, sponsors of the Tuscan team. We had seats between the sponsor and the Pistoia chairman and up to the start of the match the conversation was quite friendly. Unfortunately, after a good start Fortitudo were soon in trouble and we were soundly and compre hensively beaten. I went very silent and fortunately my wife tried to save face at least with some clever public relations . . .

My passion, however, never leads me to go over the top towards the people who are in charge of the game. I am and I will always be a referee, always trying to understand the work and the role of the man with a whistle in his mouth who is there to make sure the rules are applied correctly.

At least I try to be that way, and I have to bite my tongue at moments. It's only natural that sometimes certain words might slip out of a supporter's mouth.

Family

I met my wife in 1988, in Versilia. We fell in love and started living together almost from the very beginning. First in Bologna for a couple of years and then, after a really cold winter and an incredible snowfall one 19 April, came the decision, more hers than mine, to move to Viareggio. It was a good choice because today I can't imagine myself living anywhere else, and certainly not in a place that isn't by the sea.

My wife Gianna and my daughters, Francesca Romana and Carolina, are the most important things that I have, there's no doubt about that, even though when it's expressed like this it sounds a little clichéd.

I think that a lot of what a man manages to do with his life, the things he manages to achieve, depends on his family. The family environment, the help you can receive from someone who is continually close to you, this is something you can't get anywhere else – I really believe this. Every important decision I take is taken together with my wife, and everyone around me is totally involved. I have to admit that I've been incredibly lucky: I have a wonderful family, a family I'm proud of. This luck comes from far off in my past because the family I come from – and I'm still very close to them, to the point where my father and my mother followed me to Viareggio when we moved there from Bologna – gave me a lot and helped me to appreciate certain values, to give the right importance to certain things. And I am infinitely grateful to them for that.

My family is quite special in terms of its component parts – the female presence is certainly dominant, something I tried to correct, in vain, by introducing Wallace, a Westie terrier, strictly male . . .

I have to admit, however, that I am very happy. To tell the truth, I was keen on having a son, but now I'm convinced that having two daughters is a wonderful thing, something that brings with it moments of complete sweetness.

The fact of being surrounded by women, who don't have any particular involvement in football, helps me in my work because it's easier for me to take a break from the environment and from talk about football when I feel the need to do so. Francesca and Carolina are not likely to want to follow in my footsteps in sporting terms, something that with a son might have caused a few problems. I'm of the opinion that children's choices regarding their own futures should always be respected, but there's no doubt that a refereeing son would have approached a career similar to my own in some sort of antagonistic way. This is one more reason for being particularly happy about my two daughters.

Time off

Given the importance of my family, I try in every way to avoid stealing time from my wife and daughters. When I'm asked how I spend my time off, it's only natural that my first thoughts should go to them. My women are my hobby, I dedicate to them all the energy that I don't use in my refereeing work. I'm also lucky in that my wife and I manage to make our time off coincide. She has a shop on the seafront in Viareggio and Saturdays and Sundays are important days for her. Gianna's day off is by tradition Monday and with my work being concentrated on Saturday and Sunday, I try to keep Monday as free as possible from commitments, so as to be able to spend the whole day with her. Whenever I happen to referee on a Saturday I get a real treat because that way I get to spend Sunday with the kids and Monday with my wife.

Although I don't have any specific hobbies, I do have many interests. Above all else I love reading, which also helps me fill my time before matches, especially when I'm travelling around Italy or the world. When you're travelling like that there are many dead moments and a good book helps a lot.

I have a good relationship with the television, in the sense that I don't mind spending time in front of the screen. Obviously I prefer sport, football above all else, but basketball, athletics and cycling as well. And then I enjoy all types of films, especially thrillers and comedies.

Music is less important to me than reading – I listen to it, it keeps me company and it helps me pass the time while I'm driving. I also often have it in the background while I'm doing something else. In essence I'm a 'passive' consumer of music. Depending on my mood I can move easily from Ramazzotti to Queen, from opera to Eminem. This is quite different from my wife's approach; every time we get in the car together she makes me listen to more demanding music, often hard rock which my youngest daughter – a real fan of Aerosmith – also enjoys. They're a great group, it's just that my daughter is only eight . . .

One of the most beautiful memories of my life is related to music. There was a spectacular production of *Aida* at the Arena in Verona: I'd met Gianna two days previously and perhaps in truth I remember more of her than I do of *Aida*.

Travelling is another thing I really enjoy, or rather I would enjoy. I don't mean travelling for work, obviously, because the kilometres I travel every year in a car or on a plane are truly endless, and I can't think of that as enjoyment.

Enjoyment would be going away with my family, but it's difficult because of the calendars both my wife and myself are tied to. Between my footballing commitments, the girls' school commitments and my wife's shop, it's not easy to find the time for a trip together. We're hoping that the proposal for a three-week suspension of the championship over Christmas is confirmed and then in the future it'll be easier to have some extra days for relaxation, preferably with warm weather because I hate the cold and a holiday on the snow would really be an ordeal for me. On these occasions we travel to the Canary Islands, to Playa de las Americas where my wife's mother lives and where the weather is splendid even at Christmas.

Apart from this, unfortunately, there isn't much time at all for travelling. For example last summer, after the World Cup, the most we managed was a four-day holiday on Favignana, off Sicily.

Leaving aside the more imaginative projects, I have to admit that my way of holidaying is extremely organized. I'm not one of those who set off saying, 'Well, let's just go and then we'll see what we come across along the way.' I like planning, organizing the details, not leaving anything to chance. Otherwise I'd have to live with the nightmare of having to stop somewhere to decide where to sleep. That would ruin a holiday for me. What I need is the chance to relax, perhaps even staying put in a holiday complex and not even stepping out of the place for a week or ten days. The sun, a book and a few newspapers and I am the happiest person in the world.

The other job

My sporting commitments aren't easily reconciled with my other job as a financial consultant. I am lucky enough – although it's luck that I made for myself because I chose to do it – to be self-employed. There are no requirements in terms of hours or actual presence, although obviously if you want any success whatsoever you need to dedicate some time to the job. Since I made the initial decision the situation has changed in the sense that back then the time required by refereeing was decidedly less. As referees we were all deeply involved in what we were doing, but not to the extent we are today. And what was easy then is becoming increasingly difficult today.

Sometimes I hear people cracking jokes about so many referees being financial or insurance consultants. The reason for this is very simple and it comes from the fact that these jobs allow them to manage their own time independently, without being accountable to anyone.

Fortunately today there are instruments that allow us to obtain information in any sort of situation: television channels dedicated to the economy and finance – Bloomberg or CNBC, for example – which can be seen throughout the world. The Internet allows you to take control of a situation in any given moment, mobile phones mean you're available wherever you are and so physically being with your client is no longer indispensable in the way it once was. But there's no doubt that I'm currently having some difficulty in doing my other job. If the trend towards increasing involvement in refereeing continues, then the time I can dedicate to my job as a financial consultant will certainly have to diminish even further .

Time isn't an elastic band that you can pull as much as you like: time has its own value, its own dimension and, as mentioned above, I am not willing to sacrifice the time I spend with my family any more than is necessary.

I don't want my wife and my daughters to pay any greater price than they already do. Therefore, if I have to make a choice between my consultancy and refereeing, I have no doubts: I'll choose refereeing.

Seven

My Champions

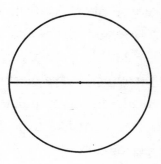

The RULES of the GAME

A Gallery of Champions

Often I'm asked the names of the footballers I admire most. The criteria I've used in choosing my 'champions' aren't only how good they are in terms of skill and class – I don't think I'm the most suitable person to discuss these things – there are so many footballers who are or have been gifted in this sense and who would merit attention.

My choice is a very personal one – related to what these champions have meant to me – linked perhaps to some particular incident, something out of the ordinary.

And I'd like to begin this sort of private gallery with a person and not a personality.

My favourite number 10 of all time was a dear friend during my university days. I was living in Bologna then, and together with my friends, all of them football fanatics, we had our own team that played what were supposedly friendlies, but which were rarely very friendly at all. We often played against the same teams over and over and so the rivalry increased and everyone played to win. The matches were usually on Saturday afternoons, on a pitch that all Bolognese people will certainly know – the 'Piccolo Paradiso' ('Little

Heaven') at Pontecchio Marconi. Those matches were so important that I would often play despite having to get in the car and drive off to referee a match on the Sunday afternoon. Obviously all of this was top secret because if the refereeing administrators in the national amateur league had known about it, I certainly would have been in trouble. But the enjoyment made it all worth it.

Our team's name was 'Cariocas' and our colours were the same as the Argentine national team. The number 10 shirt was worn by Luca Borghi, one of my best friends who unfortunately died young from cancer. In order to explain just how much he loved football and basketball, another interest that brought us together, I can tell you that after his first operation, in which one leg was amputated below the knee, he learned how to use an artificial limb and actually played again. Football and basketball meant so much to him.

Burger – that was his nickname – was a technically gifted winger, perhaps a bit slow and fancy, but for our game he was a solid reference point. I spent a lot of time with him during this part of my life and he would often make fun of me. Together with most of our friends, he couldn't quite understand my passion for refereeing. How could I spend all those weekends alone in some Italian city rather than hang around with our friends? In fact this passion of mine once meant that he had to wait for me until two in the morning – a delay in setting off for our summer holidays – just because I had to referee the final of a summer tournament in a town near Bologna. We'd planned to leave that very day, but when I was appointed to the match I didn't know how to say no. I managed to persuade Luca to delay things and so as soon as the match finished we set off for Spain, where the Italian national team had just won the World Cup. Our destination was the Costa Brava – a real 'fun-factory'. We weren't far from Barcelona and so we felt it was necessary for us to visit the Sarrià stadium. It was closed, so we simply climbed over a gate and got onto the playing surface to fetch a piece of turf that we took home as a souvenir.

But there was another thing that brought us together, and that was our physical similarity: in 1984 he was already undergoing cycles of chemotherapy, and was completely bald. It was over Christmas that year when I started losing my hair rapidly because of total alopecia, and it was with Burger and another friend of ours, Luca Castelli, that I shaved off what little hair was left on my head. The fact that Burger and I looked like each other was a great help to me in overcoming what could have been a real problem. At that time shaving one's head was not as common as it is now and our resembling each other made us both feel less different. I say made 'us' feel less different because the help I gave him was not really all that substantial – he needed much more help.

But I'd be truly happy if today, sitting up on some cloud or some star in the sky, he managed to find an answer to the question he put to me so many times back then: 'Can you explain what makes you do it?' And one of the gestures I made following the prize-giving at the Yokohama final was dedicated to him, because I'm sure he didn't miss that match.

The very first of my champions was one of my idols when I was a boy. I never refereed him, but his portrait was there in my collection of football cards. I was playing football in those days and, as an all-rounder, my favourite was Pino Wilson, captain of Lazio when they won the championship in 1973–74. This was the Lazio of Maestrelli, Chinaglia and many other greats. Wilson was a special player, both on and off the pitch – a man who always earned respect, who never gave up. Even though he didn't have a particularly imposing physique, thanks to his perfect timing he managed to fulfil his role in a way that few others have ever managed to. And he was a real character off the pitch. I remember once seeing a television interview in which he wore a pair of yellow Ray-Ban sunglasses, which for a youngster like me was the epitome of cool.

Another champion I never refereed is another great player – the greatest – Diego Armando Maradona. I started refereeing in Serie A during the 1991–92 championship, just a few months after he left Italy. Not managing to meet him on the pitch was a great disappointment because anyone who's seen him play has to recognize that he's the best of all time.

Someone I have refereed many times and whose qualities I've appreciated both as a champion on the pitch and as a man off it, is Roberto Baggio. I don't think anyone has deserved what they've got from football as much as he does, not just because of his great technical gifts, but because he's been able to recover from the serious injuries he's received. It might seem paradoxical, but it is thanks to these difficulties that he has become such a great player. If you look at his knees then you can see the marks from operations that would certainly have brought the careers of other players to an end, but he's still there, putting on a show. He's capable of recovering and starting again from scratch when it might well be easier to say enough is enough, especially if you've already won almost everything you possibly can in football. And this capacity of his for bearing the suffering means that he has earned people's love, a love that makes him everyone's champion regardless of team allegiances.

Another great, a monument to world football, is Franco Baresi. I'm tied to him by the memory of a rather special Roman afternoon. The 1993–94 season, the fifth day of the second half of the season, Roma–Milan at the Olympic Stadium, one of my first classic matches . . . and Baresi was Baresi.

Three minutes after kick-off, with Milan playing the offside trap high up the pitch, a through ball was passed to a Roma player who played it towards the Milan goal, with no opponents immediately near him and therefore, in my opinion, with a clear goal-scoring opportunity. Baresi held him back by the shirt, not dramatically, but enough to impede his progress and so I whistled for a foul.

The outcome was inevitable: a red card for Baresi in the third minute of the first half.

If the truth be told, over the following days I began to wonder if I perhaps had done him an injustice, sending him off the pitch practically without even having touched the ball. But the referee cannot and must not take into account the colours of the shirts and the names written on them. The referee has to be colour blind and has to be lacking in memory – he can't afford to recognize the players and a great champion has to have the same status on the pitch as the latest newcomer.

Coming to our own day and age, Raul Gonzales Blanco, better known simply as Raul, has a special place in my gallery of champions. Despite the fact that we've met many times for Real or Spanish national matches, the incident I'll always remember took place off the pitch. In late spring 2002 we were both at Madrid's University of Sport for the presentation of 'Footbalitis', the Adidas worldwide advertising campaign, which involved many great players such as Zidane, Rui Costa, Del Piero, Beckham, Raul as well as yours truly. We met in a corridor and said hello in front of many people, including journalists and photographers. We shook hands and then, on his part, came a hug with a kiss on the cheek – a very Latin gesture that indicates not just a formal greeting but real pleasure on seeing a person with whom one has a good relationship based on mutual respect. I appreciated the gesture and exchanged kisses. Naturally the photographers didn't let the photo-opportunity go to waste and some weeks later, on the eve of a Champions' League semi-final between Real Madrid and Barcelona, a match I was refereeing, these photographs were published by a Spanish newspaper in an attempt to present my friendship with the *madridisti* players as a scandal.

I won't make any comment on this way of attempting to exploit the incident, but I remain convinced that Raul's gesture was a demonstration of what the relationship between a player and a referee could be and ought to be. This was something that went beyond our respective roles after having known each other for many years.

For decades football was an almost exclusively male sport, but for some time now women's football has become increasingly important. For this reason I think it's right that there should be space in my gallery for a female champion, the United States player Mia Hamm. Normally it's not a very elegant thing to compare a woman to a man, but if we speak of technical ability I think it might be considered a compliment. Some years ago I did mistake Mia Hamm for a man. It was 1996 and together with a group of fellow referees I'd just arrived at Orlando, in Florida, one of the venues for the matches in the Atlanta Olympics. On the way to the organizing committee's office where our identification cards and passes were being issued, we had to walk past a pitch where at that moment a team was training. Some players were practising long shots and I remember that from far off I was particularly impressed by the power and precision of one of them. Then, as I got

nearer, came the surprise: I discovered that the team in question was the United States women's line-up and the player was
Mia Hamm.

And today I still wonder how I ever managed to mistake
her for a man.

But there is one player I'd like to mention out of a purely
subjective feeling, without recounting incidents or explaining
whys and wherefores. If I was simply responding to the question, 'Who is your favourite player?' I'd say: 'David Beckham.'

Eight

Me and . . .

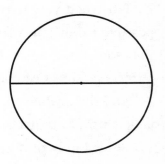

Me and . . . my hair

For many people the relationship they have with their hair is a very important one. For as long as you have it, you pay a lot of attention to it; it almost becomes a way of expressing your own personality, your own mood.

But when you start losing your hair, you do everything possible to limit the damage – using treatments and products that sometimes are only of benefit to those who sell them. Miracle products can never really be miraculous.

And then, when the situation becomes irreversible, some people turn to transplants or to wigs.

While I fully respect each individual's opinion and choice, I'm pleased that for some years now there are increasing numbers of people who when faced with baldness simply turn to the barber to have their head completely shaved.

Indeed, I find a 'billiard ball' type head more attractive than some attempts at hiding baldness, attempts that really don't hide anything.

I've already mentioned that in terms of daily life, losing my hair wasn't a problem for me. I realize, however, that in this I was extremely lucky.

Alopecia came into my life when I was twenty-four, when my character and my personality were already formed. Things would have been very different and much more difficult if this had happened earlier, perhaps in my childhood. It's difficult to explain to a child why he's not the same as others his age, and unfortunately children are very cruel in the way they focus on physical differences or imperfections.

Someone who, despite not having any hair, has managed to gain some success might become a role model for a child who suffers from alopecia.

Building confidence in a child who doesn't want to leave home without a hat covering his head, to hide something he's ashamed of, can be very useful. Showing that child there's nothing strange about not having any hair, that you can still hold your head high before millions of people, is something very beneficial.

I receive many letters, particularly from mothers, who write to me about the problems their children have and thank me for the help that I've indirectly given. Without experiencing it directly you cannot imagine how alopecia can affect people's lives. To be a role model for some of them is something that gives me pleasure and consoles me for all those times I've been called 'baldy'.

Of course, it's much more complicated to explain this to children when there are easy jokes to make about an illness that's much more widespread than anyone imagines. It might therefore be worth stopping for a moment, perhaps not looking for the easy laugh that can come from an on-the-cuff remark. It might be worthwhile to have the courage to apologize when, unthinkingly, you've hurt somebody.

But is a bald referee fit to carry out his job? Can he go out onto the pitch like any other referee or does not having hair constitute a handicap to the extent where he should limit or even give up his work?

The answer to this is obvious today, but it wasn't back in 1984 when I said goodbye to my hair for good.

Indeed, for me the answer wasn't easy and wasn't immediate. I was given a 'rest period' to see if in the meantime my hair would grow again and then, once the irreversible nature of the loss became apparent, a decision was taken to give me a trial. This was a match in Latina, where there was a particularly big crowd of some 4,000–5,000 people for the inter-regional championship, today's amateur league, a crowd that would constitute a good test.

Probably someone was worried that my appearance might make everyone laugh, but the crowd's reaction was completely normal. The supporters were there to watch a football game and that's what they did, without worrying about the length of the referee's hair.

And since then, fortunately, I've had plenty of matches with shampoo-free showers afterwards.

Me and . . . mistakes

There's a Latin saying that *errare humanum est*, to err is human, and if the ancients were saying it more than 2,000 years ago, then there must be something in it.

Another statement made by one of the greats of Italian football (and not just football) is much more recent. Giovanni Trapattoni, commenting on a terrible mistake made by his team's goalkeeper, said, 'If we have to deprive a player of the right to make mistakes, then we'd best just hang up everything and go home.'

But then again, older referees used to say, 'The best referee is the referee who makes fewest mistakes.'

So is it possible to referee a match without making mistakes? Particularly today, when television is able to show things that the human eye cannot see?

Unfortunately the answer is very simple: no.

There always have been mistakes and there always will be mistakes. It's enough just to leaf through the pages of old newspapers, even newspapers from many years ago, when the discussion was about things that were seen with the naked eye, and not about action replays. You'll find plenty in there about the mistakes made by referees back then. The so-called 'refereeing problem' was in the headlines then just as it is now.

Personally I don't believe in a technological solution or the use of slow-motion replays on the pitch. What I do believe in is the need to prepare as fully as possible in the awareness that, just as a great champion can make a mistake in taking a penalty, so can a referee make a mistake, perhaps even in giving that same penalty.

So it becomes important to know how to live with the mistake that's been made. This is particularly important during a match because sometimes a referee finds out about his mistake at half-time from live television. And even more so after the match, when the 'competition' gets under way to see who can give most emphasis to just how bad the mistake was and how much it influenced the game.

In these cases you have the disappointment of having shown yourself as not being up to the job and not having demonstrated what you'd prepared yourself to do in your training. Then added to this comes the fuss from the media's presentation of what you've done, of your mistake.

The result is that you have a difficult Sunday evening and a difficult start to the week. You'd much rather not switch on the television or read the newspapers, and try to pretend that nothing's happened.

But you can't cut yourself off completely, and it's much better to react and to show that it was simply a mistake that you could do nothing about. In this situation you always want to get back onto the pitch as soon as possible, perhaps even the next day, without having to wait a week or even longer. This is the worst moment, waiting to be appointed to another match. The same thing happens to players, although there is a big difference between us and them in terms of the consequence of a mistake. A player who has a good match and then makes a mess of a chance won't necessarily find himself on the bench the following week. A referee who after having refereed well makes an equally glaring mistake in giving a penalty, will make his kids happy the following week because he'll have all the time in the world to take them to the cinema.

As with all good moments, important achievements have to be forgotten quickly because it's crucial to keep looking forward. It's the same with mistakes, though these fade a little more slowly because you have to try to understand the reasons that led you to make the mistake. Forgetting them means not letting yourself be influenced by their memory which, in certain situations, can be a problem.

Me and . . . the report card

Collina: 6.5. A good match. Interpreted the various incidents that cropped up well.

Collina: 5. The penalty given didn't seem to be justified.

I've read so many comments like these over the days following matches I've refereed.

So do referees read the reports in the newspapers? Of course they do, there's no point denying it.

It's obvious that the judgement we're most interested in is

the judgement of those who are there to evaluate our performance; what we know about whether or not we've refereed well depends on the observer's vision of the match.

But it's equally clear that on our part there is also the curiosity about knowing whether our performance was appreciated by those who were there to report on the match.

The evaluations of our observers and the journalists don't always coincide. Indeed, sometimes there is a big difference between them as they tend to give different weight to different incidents: the observer is more concerned with the entire match, while the journalist is more interested in the individual incidents. This is because the observer is there simply to evaluate the referee and this is easier to do in terms of the whole match. The journalist, on the other hand, has to dedicate all his attention to the real protagonists of the match, the players, and the referee only comes into his picture when the referee intervenes.

Evaluating a referee's performance isn't easy, especially live, without the help of the television. It's inevitable that there can even be big differences in the journalists' interpretation of the referee. In the same match a referee may have performed well according to one journalist and poorly for another, even though the two have been sitting just a few metres apart.

I don't think a 'five' in a report card in a newspaper will ever have 'killed' anyone. While in other countries referees are not usually judged, unless they do something outrageous, in Italy it's quite normal to write and to talk about them, especially, I must say, in negative terms. Unfortunately good refereeing makes less news than a serious mistake.

I'm not complaining about being criticized or receiving negative reports – that's part of the game and it happens to players as well. The important thing is not to give it too much importance, not to let yourself be affected by it, but to use these things as a stimulus to do better. It's also important, though, that certain limits are imposed, that people remember that above and beyond the referee there's also a man there with a private life that merits respect. I'm referring to the second jobs we all do and even more so to our families, children in particular, who certainly aren't overly pleased on reading certain comments. Before using particularly harsh adjectives to describe a particularly negative performance, it might be worth stopping to think a little.

Me and . . . the action replay

In October 1967 when Carlo Sassi and Heron Vitaletti 'invented' the action replay during the sports programme *Domenica Sportiva* (*Sporting Sunday*), showing slowed-down images of an incident in a match, I'm sure they never thought it would become as important as it has done over the years.

At that time matches were filmed by a couple of cameras and the images were almost never good enough to be able to compete with the referee.

Very few incidents – only the most important – were ever shown. Over the years the technology has progressed tremendously and the television cameras are now able to show almost everything that takes place on the pitch. If you consider that Serie A matches are filmed by at least a dozen cameras and the most important matches, or Champions' League matches, are covered by sixteen to twenty cameras, the 'competition' between referee and television really is balanced in favour of the latter.

Just to give an example, during corner kicks or free kicks, television shows players being held and pushed, sometimes even in a spectacular way. These things happen inside the penalty area and people wonder how the referee can fail to spot them. Only in rare cases is it explained that these aren't the images that are broadcast live, they are, in fact, images that refer back to the action of some seconds previously. While the main cameras cover the entire penalty area, others are personalized, covering individual players or pairs of players. This means that if something happens then it's easy to spot and then broadcast it.

Unfortunately, the referee doesn't have this ability, his eyes aren't like a fly's that can focus on several images at once. His vision is global and his sensibility leads him to concentrate on certain risky situations, such as those in which a player is more concerned about his opponent than about the direction from which the ball is coming. I'm sorry to have to say it, but there is no competition between the referee and the television camera, it's like trying to go faster than a Ferrari when you're in a family saloon: you might be an excellent driver, but you can only do so much. The important thing is that whoever is driving the Ferrari knows what he's doing . . .

Many people suggest that television ought to be introduced onto the pitch, as happens for special situations in the NFL and the NBA, the American professional football and basketball leagues. But there are substantial differences between soccer and these sports that come with their inevitable interruptions, which are useful for commercial television. This is particularly true of American football, which in many respects is a sport 'created' for television. In any case I'd like to point out how the television replay is used only in very particular circumstances. In NBA basketball, for example, its use is limited to shots made just as time is running out, to judge the position of the ball against the timekeeper's watch and where it was with respect to the player's hands at that moment – sometimes a matter of hundredths of a second, impossible for a human eye to catch.

Apart from these considerations, fortunately I am a referee and therefore it's not up to me to decide whether the help of television is a road we should go down or not, but I do have a couple of things to say.

First, it's not true at all that referees are generally against the action replay because this would mean 'relinquishing power': for a referee on the pitch the last thing he's interested in is power and in any case, even when using this instrument, the final decision would be his.

Secondly, I think it's important to underline the beauty

of this sport in which the same rules apply in the most important of stadiums and in the smallest of pitches in the outskirts.

It's true, referees make mistakes and these mistakes can sometimes influence the result of a match, but often referees are not the only people to make mistakes.

Players make mistakes too, as do the managers on the benches. But perhaps their mistakes are different from ours. Perhaps they're allowed to make mistakes while we're not.

I don't want to hear anyone saying that players 'pay' for their mistakes, because that's exactly what happens to us as well.

I think there is a tendency to exaggerate the idea of television as being the repository of absolute truth. If the images show something that contrasts with the referee's vision, the guilty verdict is issued immediately and without any mitigation. The really incredible thing is that if the images don't show what the referee actually saw, and this does sometimes happen, then rather than believing him and accepting the decision, he is assumed to have been wrong because there are no images to support his decision.

This is what happened during the 1998 World Cup in France to the American referee, Esfandiar Baharmast, after the Norway–Brazil game. The match was a decisive one, not for Brazil who had already qualified, but for Morocco, who were competing with Norway for second place. The teams were drawing 1-1 when a penalty was given to Norway because of a foul – a foul that the television cameras failed to pick-up.

The penalty was scored, Norway won, and consequently qualified. Furious arguments then ensued in the newspapers and
on television, accusing the stronger footballing continents of
inflicting a disservice on the poorer continents – all of this
based on the assumption that the decision was wrong. For two
days I lived through this together with Baharmast and I saw at
first hand his frustration at not being believed. He endured
two days of sheer hell until the images produced by one of the
Scandinavian channels showed that, off the ball, the Brazilian,
Junior Baiano, had in fact held Tore Andre Flo by the shirt, so
the decision made on the pitch had been correct.

Even though Baharmast was vindicated thanks to these
images, who will ever be able to repay him for those two
hellish days he lived through?

It's completely unthinkable today to attempt to wage
war against television, it wouldn't make any sense. What we
have to do is find a way of living with it. I believe the
only possible way of doing this is to accept that there is one
match played on a pitch with its own facts – those perceived
by the players, trainers, assistants, referee and supporters –
and another that happens at the same time – the match shown
by television, that has its own facts which might be slightly
different from the other game. This does not make it any less
real because of this, just simply different.

Taken this way, the replay might be very useful, not to
'uncover' the referee's mistakes, but to help the referee
improve.

What sense is there in using a shot, for example, taken

from a camera positioned behind the goal, a location inaccessible to the referee during the match, and then ask the same referee to base his decision on it?

To say that referees are performing poorly just because an image, perhaps taken from an angle diametrically opposite that of the referee, shows that a mistake had been made, is not only wrong, but it does nothing to help referees improve.

Understanding why a specific mistake was made through analysis of images is the only way of ensuring growth and of trying to avoid the same mistake being made again.

Me and . . . doping

The referee is the rules man, the man who goes onto the pitch to make sure the rules are respected and help the two teams play the match in full respect of the rules. It's clear that on this basis respect for the rules really does become part of the referee's mindset and therefore the mere idea of using fraudulent means to achieve a sporting goal cannot form part of my way of seeing things.

Respect for the rules and respect for one's opponents, respect for the efforts made and the energies used by your opponents in preparing for the competition.

Doping, the use of substances that allow you to obtain results superior to those your physique would normally achieve, is above all else a lack of respect for others.

It's right that the use of substances that cause damage to one's own body should be prosecutable and punishable by the law, but for me this isn't the important point. Paradoxically, and I am aware that this statement takes things to extremes, I could even accept that someone might decide to ruin themselves for personal pleasure, to prove simply to themselves that they are capable of doing something that their body would otherwise never manage to do, but always in contexts that do not involve competition. Indeed, smoking and drinking alcohol in large quantities doesn't do people's health any good, but nobody's prosecuted and punished for doing that.

What is not acceptable is using chemistry to improve one's own performance and win a competition to the detriment of those who have trained using only hard work and sweat.

The final result has to be achieved through what one's own body is capable of doing and the improvements made must be the fruit of daily training, commitment and sacrifice. It's too easy, and at the same time too risky, to seek shortcuts for obtaining the same result with no effort. And precisely because the greatest risks are run by young people, the example that top sporting people can give is of fundamental importance.

Rigorous, carefully controlled, strict and regulated punishments are the means for making sure that the cases that have come to light in recent years are not repeated. But this work has to be backed up with a widespread programme of sports education, to make people understand just how satisfying it is to practise sport and how competition is a way of putting oneself to the test in a clean way, without any dirty tricks.

Me and . . . my memories

As I've already mentioned, while you're still working, while you're still a 'referee on the pitch', you cannot and must not look back and think about what you've achieved.

It's much more important to continue looking forward, to the future, towards all that you still have to do in getting ready as best as possible for the future, leaving the memories for the moment when you retire.

I'm not a photography enthusiast and so I don't travel the world armed with a camera, immortalizing moments and situations for future memory.

And so, when the day comes when I can reflect freely on what I've done, on the matches I've refereed, I'm sure my collection of players' shirts will be a great help.

It might seem a bit childish, but I'm convinced that the best memory, the truest memory of a match refereed are the shirts of the players who played in that match, even more so today now that the shirts are all personalized.

I have some truly special items in my collection, above all else the shirt Ronaldo wore in the World Cup final in Yokohama. And then Dieter Hamann's from the same match, Jaap

Stam and Mehmet Scholl's from the Champions' League final between Manchester United and Bayern Munich, Zinedine Zidane's from France–Spain in Euro 2000.

My daughter Carolina has taken possession of the shirt Beckham wore in the match against Argentina in the last World Cup and there's no way of getting it back from her.

I've also inserted a few of the shirts I used in the more important matches into the collection – recognition I decided to grant myself because I felt as though I was also one of the protagonists of those finals.

After all, the referee's shirt does arouse a certain interest and players often ask me for it at the end of a match. I think this is positive and illustrates the good relations that can exist on the pitch. Unfortunately, unlike the players, we don't receive a great number of strips at the beginning of each season and although I run the risk of sounding a bit mean, I have to explain that if I were to give them the shirt then I'd have to referee the next match naked.

The collection consists not just of shirts, there are also balls, but not many. Managing to take them home isn't easy, especially after the World Cup final. We were just seconds away from the end of the match, with the result already clear, and I started thinking about how to make sure the ball didn't disappear. To do what the Brazilian referee Coelho did in the 1982 final when Italy won – blowing the whistle as he lifted the ball above his head – seemed a bit too much, but I had to make sure I got hold of it somehow. So I started getting closer to the Brazilian player who was in possession at that moment, telling him in Spanish, since I have no Portuguese, to pass me the ball. Perhaps because of the excitement, he didn't understand and thus we began a strange sort of chase with time already over. Those who know a bit about refereeing will certainly have noticed it and then, thanks to a foul committed by a German player, I managed to get to the ball and, after having picked it up, I blew the final whistle. And throughout the post-match period, including the prize-giving, it remained in my hands because there was a real risk that it might disappear.

Me and . . . advertising

I was very surprised the first time an agency contacted me to invite me to take part in an advertising campaign.

Up until then – it was spring 2000, and I feel as though a century has passed since then – no company had ever turned to a referee to help promote its image.

To tell the truth, a few years previously, as part of the technical sponsorship of the Italian Referees' Association, Diadora had obtained permission to use my picture for a series of advertisements based on this relationship.

Above and beyond the advantages of participating in this, especially from the economic point of view (but it's not as lucrative as you would imagine), the part of it I enjoyed most was being able to show everyone that the figure of the referee can be presented in a way that's different from the norm. No longer is the referee 'a necessary evil for the game of football', but now he is someone who can project an image to the public and therefore produce an extremely positive view of the referee's role. Certainly the other people involved in that campaign with me all have very positive images, from Yuri Chechi to Cino Ricci, from Luciano De Crescenzo to Oliviero Toscani, all of them great figures in their fields.

Contributing towards a positive image of the referee is of fundamental importance not only at the top level, at the professional level, but also, and most importantly, at the bottom level – youth and amateur football, where very often, too often, the referee is alone, too alone.

And it was this feeling of solitude that I was referring to in the 2002 Adidas campaign when I described what it feels like to walk onto the pitch.

Five seconds, the time it takes to walk up the steps
that lead to the pitch.
And then you're alone in the midst of thousands of
people . . .